The Assertive Woman

the Assertive Woman

New Edition for a New Millennium!

Stanlee Phelps
Nancy Austin
Co-Author · *A Passion for Excellence*

The Bestselling Assertiveness Book for Women
Revised and Updated for the 21st Century

Impact Publishers®
SAN LUIS OBISPO, CALIFORNIA 93406

Editions
First Edition, 1975, Second Edition, 1987
Third Edition, 1997
Copyright © 1970, 1987, 1997
by Stanlee Phelps and Nancy Austin
Second Printing, September, 1997

ATTENTION ORGANIZATIONS AND CORPORATIONS:

This book is available at quantity discounts on bulk purchases for educational, business, or sales promotional use. For further information, please contact Impact Publishers, P.O. Box 1094, San Luis Obispo, CA 93406 (Phone: 1-800-246-7228).

Library of Congress Cataloging-in-Publication Data

Phelps, Stanlee.
 The assertive woman / Stanlee Phelps, Nancy Austin. — 3rd ed.
  p.   cm.
 Includes bibliographical references and index.
 ISBN 1-886230-05-6
 1. Assertiveness in women. 2. Women—Life skills guides.
 3. Feminism—United States.   I. Austin, Nancy. II. Title.
 HQ1206.P44   1997
 155.6'33—dc21   97-2908
                                                   CIP

Impact Publishers and colophon are registered trademarks of Impact Publishers, Inc.

Printed in the United States of America on acid-free paper
Cover designed by Sharon Schnare, San Luis Obispo, California

Published by **Impact ♲ Publishers®**
POST OFFICE BOX 1094
SAN LUIS OBISPO, CALIFORNIA 93406

Dedication

...in loving memory of my mother, Connie Phelps
---- Stanlee Phelps

...and to Marilyn Austin, with much love.
---- Nancy Austin

Contents

Acknowledgements

Sometimes, writing a new edition is a simple matter of adding and subtracting material and changing a few dates. In this case, a whole new book has evolved over the years as the assertive woman herself has evolved. With respect and tender acknowledgement for being a symbol of transformation from demure to assertive, we have retired the image of Mona Lisa, which graced the covers of former editions. This new Third Edition is preparation for the challenges and choices of the 21st century.

To our families and dear friends, we express our heartfelt thanks. Their contributions, love and unconditional support helped us produce our best efforts.

We also want to express our sincere appreciation to the hundreds of women who have participated in our seminars. We thank them for their willingness to tell us about their adventures as assertive women. And to the women and men who made a special effort to complete the Feedback section in the first edition, and to those who wrote us personal letters, we want you to know that we could not have finished this book without you. Though we have never met, you have been a most important source of inspiration throughout. Thank you.

Bob Alberti, our friend and publisher, has enthusiastically encouraged us from the beginning. His never-give-up attitude sustained us, and for that and his warmth, we thank him. Melissa Alberti Froehner and Sharon Skinner too, have been troopers! We thank them for their time, care, and sense of crafts-womanship. We gratefully acknowledge the other staff members at Impact Publishers as well — for doing everything from getting packages to us overnight, to answering the telephone on the first ring, to always sounding happy to hear from us. Their work shines through on every page of *The Assertive Woman*.

And to our new readers, a very special welcome. We trust this is the beginning of a beautiful relationship!

S.P.
N.A.
April 1997

Chapter 1

Introduction

Adventure is worthwhile in itself.
---- Amelia Earhard

This third edition of *The Assertive Woman* looks forward to the promise of a new century, and a new millennium. From the beginning, this book has been a faithful guide and source of inspiration to women everywhere. We trust it will become an important part of your life, too. Readers have told us that *The Assertive Woman*, like a friend they can always count on, has helped them find and follow their dreams at home, at work, and at play.

You may be reading this book for the first time. Perhaps your goal is to fortify your self-confidence. Or maybe you want to make your mark in the world and don't know where to begin. We offer answers based on twenty years of practice and the collected experiences of thousands of women who found the nerve and the happy chance to fulfill their dreams.

We have a lot to cheer about! Since our first edition appeared in bookstores twenty years ago, unparalleled opportunities have opened up for women. We have taken our places as bishops and astronauts, veejays and professional basketball players, movie producers and chief executives. An overwhelming number of us have done it while having children and raising families and caring for aging parents. Working moms and "mompreneurs" are no longer a novelty; we're the norm. This book has something to say to one and all.

The best news, though, is that the old idea of an assertive woman
---- a shrew who would rise up from years of oppression and make life
miserable for everyone ---- has been utterly discredited. Assertiveness is
the collagen of daily life, a powerful connective tissue that enriches
relationships, opens doors, and strengthens bonds. It will never go out of
style, no matter the century ---- or millennium.

How to Use This Book as a Workbook

Throughout this book, exercises have been included for you to
complete. Some of these require only a written response, and others
involve actually trying on new behaviors. We have used each and every
one of the exercises in our workshops and find them to be enormously
effective aids to learning assertive behavior.

We suggest that you do each exercise in the order in which it is
presented. Some are designed for you to do alone. Others are intended
to be completed with a friend, and several work best when used as group
exercises.

*The exercise pages may be copied for use in groups or workshops, provided
they are not sold commercially, and that credit is given. Please refer to the
copyright notice, page iv.*

Do You Know Your AQ?

If you're asking yourself, "What will I gain by reading *The Assertive
Woman?*" begin by testing your assertiveness quotient (AQ). Use this scale
to indicate how comfortable you are with each item:

1 ---- makes me very uncomfortable
2 ---- I feel moderately comfortable
3 ---- I am very comfortable with this

There may be some situations which don't apply to you; in those
cases, try to imagine how comfortable you would be if you were involved
in the situation.

By the way, some of our workshops have included men, who have
often found it enlightening to test their own assertiveness and to compare
their responses to those of women they know. The AQ can be a
non-threatening way to spark conversation.

1-2-3

BECOMING ASSERTIVE
- Speaking up and asking questions at a meeting.   _____
- Commenting about being interrupted by a man directly to him at the moment he interrupts you.   _____
- Stating your views to a male authority figure (e.g., minister, boss, therapist, father).   _____
- Presenting ideas and elaborating on them when there are men present.   _____

THE INNER GAME OF ASSERTIVENESS
- Using your inner wisdom to guide you in making clear decisions instead of doing what someone else thinks you should do.   _____
- Going out with a group of friends when you are the only one without a "date."   _____
- Being especially competent, using your authority and/or power without labeling yourself as bitchy, impolite, bossy, aggressive, castrating, or parental.   _____
- Requesting expected service when you haven't received it (e.g., in a restaurant or a store).   _____

OBSTACLES ON THE PATH TO ASSERTIVENESS
- Laughing at or ignoring the negative chatter in your head that reinforces old beliefs and prevents you from taking assertive risks.   _____

COMPASSION TRAP
- Choosing to do what is right for you without guilt, in spite of another's manipulations.   _____
- Respecting your own needs at least as much as you do others.'   _____

EMPOWERING YOURSELF TO BE ASSERTIVE
- Taking time every day increase your power and confidence.   _____
- Being expected to apologize for something and *not* apologizing since you feel you are right.   _____
- Requesting the return of borrowed items without being apologetic.   _____

1-2-3

EXPRESSION OF ASSERTION
- Confidently using assertive expression that fits your own unique style and personality — not aiming for "perfection."   _____
- Recognizing the difference between genuine assertiveness and its imitations: Pollyanna Assertion, Fraudulent Assertion, and Reckless Assertion.   _____
- Respecting the limits of assertion and preventing the Superwoman Syndrome.   _____

YOU'RE WORTH IT
- Talking about your talents and triumphs openly without embarrassment.   _____
- Looking in the mirror with a genuine smile and saying to yourself out loud, "I really like you. You're O.K. in my book."   _____

ASSERTIVE BODY IMAGE
- Entering and exiting a room where men are present.   _____
- Speaking in front of a group.   _____
- Maintaining eye contact, keeping your head upright, and leaning forward when engaged in conversation.   _____

COMPLIMENTS, CRITICISM, AND REJECTION
- Receiving a compliment by saying something assertive to acknowledge that you agree.   _____
- Accepting a rejection.   _____
- Not getting the *approval* of the most significant male in your life, or of *any* male.   _____
- Discussing another person's criticism of you openly with that person.   _____
- Telling someone that she/he is doing something that is bothering you.   _____

1-2-3

SAYING "NO"
- Refusing to get coffee or to take notes at a meeting where you are chosen to do so because you are female. _____
- Saying "no" ~~ refusing to do a favor when you really don't feel like it. _____
- Turning down a request for a meeting or date. _____

MANIPULATION
- Telling a person when you think she/he is manipulating you. _____
- Commenting to a man who has made a patronizing remark to you (e.g., "you have a good job *for a woman*"; "you're not flighty/emotional/stupid/hysterical *like most women*"). _____

SENSUALITY
- Telling a prospective lover about your physical attraction to him/her before any such statements are made to you. _____
- Initiating sex with your partner. _____
- Showing physical enjoyment of an art show or concert in spite of others' reactions. _____
- Asking to be caressed and/or telling your lover what feels good to you. _____
- Negotiating with a prospective lover for "safe sex" that insures against sexually-transmitted diseases. _____

ANGER
- Expressing anger directly and honestly when you feel angry. _____
- Arguing with another person. _____

HUMOR
- Telling a joke. _____
- Listening to a friend tell a story about something embarrassing, but funny, that you have done. _____
- Responding with humor to someone's put-down of you.

1-2-3

FRIENDS AND LOVERS

- Speaking and making a request for emotional support and understanding from a friend. _____
- Letting go of old friends and making new friends when it is appropriate to do so. _____
- Risking rejection an feeling foolish in a romantic relationship. _____
- Taking positive action to face fear and conflict in your relationships. _____

FAMILY RELATIONSHIPS

- Approaching your relationship with your parents more honestly and openly. _____
- Disciplining your own children. _____
- Disciplining others' children. _____
- Explaining the facts of life or your divorce to your child. _____

ASSERTIVENESS AT WORK

- Initiating a discussion with your boss about a raise or opportunity for promotion. _____
- Refusing to do your boss's personal errands or shopping. _____
- Accepting performance feedback from your boss, especially when it concerns the need to improve in some area. _____
- Pushing for employer-sponsored day care programs. _____

THE MYTHOLOGY OF THE WORKING WOMAN

- Debunking the most common myths about working women: they are too emotional, too insecure, not professional enough. _____
- Knowing the difference between a Superwoman and a super woman. _____
- Speaking up when you or another woman is accused of being "too emotional" to be effective. _____
- Being able to say no when asked to take on one more extra project "for the sake of your career." _____

THE HARDY SPIRIT
- Accepting a challenge and sticking with it.   _____
- Picking up that hobby or special interest which was
  abandoned earlier in life.   _____
- Taking a courageous stand, either personally or politically.   _____

Though our AQ Survey is not a validated psychological test, it can help you decide how to approach assertiveness, and where to begin. If you have mostly 1's and 2's under a particular heading, be sure to give special attention to the corresponding chapter. If you have more 1's and 2's throughout the AQ Survey than you do 3's, *The Assertive Woman* can help you to express yourself more spontaneously and honestly. For those of you who have fifty or more 3's ⸺ congratulations! You already are an assertive woman. We especially recommend Chapter 24, "Same Song, *Third* Verse" and putting your assertiveness to work for yourself in a larger context.

Although our book is intended to be read in sequence, you may want to concentrate on some areas that relate more to your individual needs, as highlighted by your AQ score. After reading *The Assertive Woman* and completing the exercises, test your AQ again to see how much your responses have changed.

We've also described lots of situations that call for assertiveness. You may find some of them unrealistic; we recognize that life does not march ahead smoothly and neatly. We hope you'll recognize the limitations of space and forgive us if the situations seem too easily resolved. They are included not as models of "how to succeed at assertion without really trying," but to illustrate how the process can be applied. When someone leaps off the printed page and confronts you for real, you may need to persist longer and stand firmer. When your assertiveness is wholeheartedly welcomed, of course, it can be a piece of cake. Part of the process is the experience of each.

Chapter 2

Our Personal Journeys

Stanlee Phelps

You teach best what you most need to learn.
---- Richard Bach, *Illusions*

The First Edition of *The Assertive Woman* was published in 1975. At that time assertiveness was an exciting revolutionary concept for me. It is still exciting.

For the most part my personal journey has been exhilarating and rewarding. Yet, identifying and creating assertive choices has been difficult too. The price paid for keeping my options alive was not always worth it. And, being labeled an expert in assertion did not help. I often felt pressure to live up to what I had put into print.

I wanted to be a model for others. Indeed, there were times when I could actually do that. At other times I pretended while I disintegrated inside. Later I learned it was O.K. not to be assertive at times. In fact, sometimes I did not *want* to be assertive.

There were other possibilities. For example, if I chose to be passive, or if I chose to be aggressive, the act of *choosing* was still assertive when I took responsibility for the consequences of my choice. I was not locked into assertiveness as just another thing I "should" or "must" do. I could be human instead of an assertiveness robot!

I had mini-triumphs ---- returning damaged merchandise, saying "no" to telemarketers, delegating more, accepting compliments and other things I could proudly label "assertive." However, it was not as smooth and easy asserting myself with significant people in my life.

It became increasingly evident to me that real assertion had to begin inside me. My goal was to clarify my values, my likes and dislikes, and most of all —— to become comfortable with my inner self. The assertive woman inside of me knew what to do. I had to *open* to what she was telling me.

Besides growing confidence how did I know this was working? I needed to test it outwardly in the laboratory of my life.

The first test was changing careers from clinical work and teaching to corporate consulting. It was risky letting go of financial security and my professional identity. To step out into the entrepreneurial unknown took courage. Having a sense of humor and a "hardy spirit" helped, especially as I made my second major career transition to become an executive for one of the largest career services firms in the world.

Relationships have always tested me the most. Trusting myself and the simple rules of assertion gave me room to grow. I made the most progress with men, especially when I began to see them more realistically. Images of supermen that remained strong for me, the damsel in distress, regardless of how they were feeling, were retired. Today I enjoy relating to assertive, not aggressive, men who appreciate assertive women. I employ compassion, confrontation and humor with those who are not assertive.

More fulfilling than ever, my relationships with women continue to blossom. Much of my work is aimed at advancing quality lives for all women and the men and children they love. I have deepened my individual friendships with women. One of the most powerful ways has been through my dedicated participation in ongoing support groups. In these groups we share career changes, marriages, adoptions, triumphs, losses and hormones of horror.

In recent years I have had to learn how to be an assertive caregiver. As a caregiver the lines can blur easily between falling into a Compassion Trap and giving from a healthy perspective. Two very real situations come to mind:

My step-brother contracted the AIDS virus. When his condition worsened, he was forced to stop working and a friend moved in to care for him. I arranged to relieve his friend and hospice workers on weekends. His physical presence was frightening and he was withdrawn emotionally and spiritually. Comforting him and leading him to peace was the gift I wanted to give him. Because he was unable to express his feelings, I became his voice and recalled for him both the terrific and tragic times of his life. For weeks he tentatively clung to life as I gave him permission to let go of his suffering. When he died I felt fortunate that I had been a healthy caregiver and had not relinquished my own needs.

Another time to be the major caregiver was in store for me. Following my mother's eightieth birthday, she broke her leg ⸺ the beginning of an irreversible decline. After surgery she needed rehabilitation and daily assistance. She hated being in a board-and-care home even though it was temporary. She returned home, but in time became unable to function independently. Her memory faltered and her ability to maintain her daily routine fell apart. My responsibilities expanded to include the hiring, firing and management of home health care workers. Near Mom's eighty-first birthday she broke her wrist, rendering her more handicapped. The most agonizing, but best, decision was to move her to an assisted living residence for seniors. The last months of her life were spent in dignity and nurturing. Our relationship was freed to enjoy one another's company. If I had given in to her wish to remain home and continued to manage the ever increasing demands, we would not have had precious and fun times together. For me, the ability to reach out to other family members, friends and community resources was a true act of assertion.

In my relationship with Greg, my husband, I've had more opportunities to test my assertiveness skills. An intimate relationship with a life partner often requires one to risk revealing innermost desires and hurts in order to grow together in aliveness. We've come face-to-face with issues on power, sex, money, jobs, relatives, friends, pets, parents, politics, time, eating, exercise, home repair, bad habits, broken promises and a whole host of things as silly as fighting over the types of cucumbers that make good pickles. We often comment on how grateful we are to be able to communicate openly with each other.

My story wouldn't be complete without acknowledging the delightful ways in which my two puppies, Dash and Phoebe, have enriched my journey. Because I was physically unable to have children and chose not to adopt, my puppies are my kids. In fact, I've compared notes with "real" moms only to find many shared joys and frustrations of parenting. When I'm with them the good news and the bad news is that I don't focus on myself. For example, taking Dash and Phoebe to Puppy Kindergarten (a class for dogs and their owners) is quite an adventure. The dogs are supposed to be learning how to get along with other breeds and a diversity of people, but I'm convinced that it's really an assertive training class in disguise for us, the inept parents!

My journey is not over. I look forward to the anticipated, as well as the unforeseen, events that arise as occasions to fine-tune my assertiveness skills and behavior. When I'm referred to as an "assertive woman," I feel a real sense of pride and accomplishment. I hope you do too.

The feedback and encouragement that we've received from our readers has enabled us to add to recent editions about what life has been like for other assertive women. I would enjoy hearing from you personally. What you've encountered in your journey has meaning for us all.

Nancy K. Austin

"DO IT NOW."
~ Signature management motto
of Warnaco Group CEO Linda Wachner

The year Stanlee and I wrote *The Assertive Woman*, we knew who she was: honest, direct, courageous. Nobody's fool. A woman who could make her own way and turns her own corners. She can say "no" to unreasonable demands. She can declare her love (and be loved back). Now, more than two decades later, that image is as appealing as ever. Yet for me, starting out, the promise of being an assertive woman triggered a lot of new questions.

I've reread the book (well, certain chapters, anyway) when I started business school, when I became a stepmother, when I had to untwist a complex problem or get through a rocky meeting at work. It always makes me want to hang in when I'd rather check out. It has had the noble capacity to encourage ("to stimulate by assistance or approval," the dictionary says), to push me toward what is best confronted squarely. Even if it's only getting out of bed when the alarm goes, it seems a daring act against an assertive landscape.

But here's the thing. Unlike a book, my own life has not marched so neatly. Against our own well-balanced advice, I didn't master the cinchy stuff before going on to the real gut-wrenchers. I've marveled at how "real" assertive women do it. Where do they get their nerve?

I never needed assertiveness more, though, than when I entered UCLA's MBA program. We women first-years felt extra pressure to show we could cut it. It wasn't just *our* careers that were at stake, but those of other women who would depend on our performance. People were watching us (this was back when we were actually called "trailblazers" and "pioneers") and how we did. To show that we belonged, that our very existence was noncontingent and just get used to it, okay?, the student-run organizations in B-School were positively studded with women. We had Women in Management, Women in Banking, Women in Computers, Women Everywhere. We had someplace to go, things to do, people to see. Of course we belonged.

So did the men, but then nobody pestered them with dopey questions about how they would keep their emotions under wraps at work (read: don't cry), and especially how they planned to achieve "balance in their lives." No need, since that answer was obvious to everyone: it's a woman's job. I don't think anybody even considered the possibility that he might do some extra wifing, even though his wife (with her own career to worry about) could have used a wife herself.

Out of school and in the job market, my assertive skills were continually tested. Sometimes higher-ups were put off by that "assertive woman" label. More often, though, colleagues and bosses were mightily reassured when they saw that assertiveness did not mean I would bite their heads off. Nor was I, as some feared (and I quote): a "TLB" (tough little broad). On the contrary. There were a couple of meetings when I was so afraid of being thought overwhelming and threatening that I hunkered down in my corner and kept a lower profile than was actually constructive — but no one could say I was bitchy! Oh, and I let my sense of humor show. When a man with whom I worked shoulder-to-shoulder for four years joked that my next book should be *The Assertive Woman's Cookbook*, I really thought it was funny, coming from Ray, that is — whose genuine respect for me and my work came through loud and clear every day.

I see I have neglected to mention that back when I began my second year of graduate school, I did it with a husband, a house, and an eight-year-old stepson. We've been married twenty years now, and the eight-year-old kid is a successful television sports anchor. I've worked for a Fortune 50 company (and loved it), a monster accounting firm (a mistake) and a teensy consulting firm (another blunder). The companies I co-founded a dozen years ago are doing fine, as is the product of my second book partnership, A *Passion for Excellence*. I'm still chief executive of my own small company, and my husband, Bill, works with me. I work with business leaders in every industry about how leading change means changing leadership.

Most all of what I know about being assertive I've learned in real time. You can't spend four years working in a 75,000 person company and not figure out how to get things done. I have pretty much gotten to the point were I can say I am grateful for my mistakes and my wrong turns. Without them, it would have taken forever to know what I really could do well (though it's hard to think of some of those whoppers as educational).

You have to be stubborn and strong to persist, against long odds or short. That, I think, is the essence of assertiveness: at its best, it helps you crash through somebody else's idea of where you belong so you can be who you are and do what you love to do. At work, it helps you escape "sticky floors" ---- a condition that prevents rising from entry level positions into a particular career path ---- and it helps women break through the glass ceiling (no optical illusion, it's what the men in the boardroom stand on). At home, as a parent and a wife, assertiveness improves just about everything it touches. It very often smoothes the way during a rough patch, and then things even out. It adds depth and texture to a relationship. It's never boring.

Above all, assertiveness is a clarion call to action. Don't lollygag, it says, do something! Follow your wildest dream. Join the police force, go back to school, conduct a symphony. Move under your own power, in a trajectory you choose. In spite of the struggles and setbacks, it is still the best idea we ever had.

Chapter 3

Who Is The Assertive Woman?

The most important section of The Assertive Woman *was the exercise where you asked me to look in the mirror and list ten positive things about myself. I had an incredible feeling —— "I really don't know myself!"*

—— A female educational administrator,
mid-thirties and married.

R eal assertiveness doesn't happen overnight.

From hundreds of letters from readers and discussions with thousands of seminar participants, we are keenly aware of the frustration experienced by people who sincerely want to become assertive. Assertiveness does not come from a textbook, seminar, or self-help book. Real assertiveness is born within. (That's not to say, "You either have it or you don't." Rather, "If you want it, it must start with you.")

Many never understood the meaning of assertiveness in the first place: they believed, and still do, that it is just a slick cover-up for aggression. Some think that assertiveness is just a milder, "nicer" form of aggressiveness. Yet the two are entirely distinct sets of behaviors with different objectives and motivations.

Ideal vs. Real Assertiveness

Perhaps we can clear up some of the frustration and confusion by comparing the idealistic, orderly, rational process of being assertive with the chaotic, disorderly process we know you face in day to day life.

The following chart spells out some differences between ideal and real assertiveness:

<u>Ideal</u>	*vs.*	<u>Real</u>
I need to be perfectly assertive.		I'll do my best; it may not be perfect.
She/he must respond to my assertions assertively.		She/he may be passive or aggressive in response to my assertiveness.
Others must appreciate my assertions.		Others may not like my assertions.
My assertions must always achieve the desired result.		I may not always get what I want.
I must want to be always assertive.		Sometimes I won't want or care to be assertive.
I need to know what is the most assertive response at all times and implement it immediately with ease and comfort.		Sometimes I'll be confused about what's assertive, afraid, or just plain forget and revert back to old patterns.
If I blow it, I won't have another chance.		I can always try again.

A New Look at Four Women We All Know

As you begin your journey toward greater effectiveness in self-expression and relationships with others, it will help to have a framework for comparing the way you usually behave with the style you'd like to develop.

Generally, there are three ways people behave in any given situation: passive, aggressive, and assertive. As each style is described, you will probably find yourself identifying with all of them.

FOUR WOMEN WE ALL KNOW [AND THEIR MALE COUNTERPARTS]

	DORRIE DOORMAT (DAN DOORMAT)	AUGUSTA AGGRESSIVE (ARNOLD AGGRESSIVE)	ISABEL INDIRECT (IAGO INDIRECT)	ALLISON ASSERTIVE (ALEX ASSERTIVE)
Basic Attitude	I'm not okay.	You're not okay.	You're not okay, but I'll let you **think** you are.	I'm okay and you're okay, too!
Power	Feels helpless, turns power over to others, uses guilt to control.	Substitutes control and domination for power.	Uses manipulation and deceit to gain control.	Has personal power and shares power easily. Can be vulnerable.
Decision Making	Lets others choose for her.	Chooses for others whether they like it or not.	Is sneaky or deceitful in choosing for others.	Plays the inner game; chooses for herself and supports others in making their own decisions.
Potential Traps	Compassion trap. Pollyanna assertion.	Reckless assertion; super assertion; aggression trap.	Fraudulent assertion.	Superwoman trap.
Feedback from Others	Guilt, anger, frustration, lack of respect, abuse.	Fear, defensiveness, humiliation, hurt.	Suspicion, confusion, frustration; feels manipulated.	Respect, love, support, inspiration, acceptance, comfort.
Sense of Humor	Is often cruelly teased, colludes with put-downs about herself; lets others be funny.	Caustic wit, put-downs, can't laugh at herself.	Sarcasm and cynicism.	Playful, loving humor; can laugh at herself; risks being funny.
Courage	Fearful, withdraws, does not stand up for her convictions; tries to get sympathy.	Attacks and blames others to cover up her fear and insecurity. Talks "tough" and takes unwise risks.	Uses trickery and feigns other emotions (e.g. love, sadness, anger) to cover up her fear.	Is willing to deal with difficulty and pain; has the strength of her convictions; takes calculated risks.
Gains/Payoffs	Attention, sympathy, protection, doted on.	Controls people and situations; wants authority and to be right.	Sometimes seen as cute and clever; has fun playing games.	Self-respect, integrity, responsibility, freedom, intimacy.
Price Tags Paid	Loss of freedom, self-respect and creativity.	Loss of love, friendship and teamwork.	Is not trusted; is the victim of retaliation and vengeance.	Unrealistic expectations from self and others to be "perfectly" assertive.
Burnout Potential	Very high — usually depletes herself; can't say no.	Very high — overwork competition, often superachievers with physical health problems.	Very high — takes more and more energy to cover-up deceits and games.	Very high — can become too competent and accomplished from not discriminating her choices and setting limits.
Career Profile	Does what she thinks she **should** do — even if it makes her unhappy.	Often an unhappy overachiever, who may be a financial success and a person of status.	Once her untrustworthiness is discovered, her career takes a nosedive.	Usually happy and successful, she feels she can do anything she desires.
End Results	Life is a chore for the martyr.	Loneliness and bitterness.	Loss of identity, trust, and respect.	Love, happiness and peace of mind.

We have added a fourth general classification by treating aggressive behavior in two parts: direct and indirect. This distinction is important because women frequently attempt to hide or mask their aggressiveness. Being indirect is a culturally-approved choice for women, while being overtly aggressive has been reserved for men. Other authors have chosen to refer to indirect aggression as "covert aggression" or "passive-aggressive" behavior. We chose not to use "covert" since the word has an almost insidious connotation that may make women appear to have preconceived, evil intentions. We do not feel this is true, but that, in fact, women have been given little opportunity to behave in a more direct way. When one is oppressed, one learns to be subtle.

You may, like many readers of this book, want to learn how to act differently in situations where you feel trapped by your own habits. As the four styles of behavior are discussed, it will help to imagine which seem most comfortable for you and which you see as difficult. Most women identify with the passive or indirectly aggressive behaviors more than the aggressive or assertive. How do you see yourself?

PASSIVE OR NON-ASSERTIVE

In the accompanying chart, we refer to the passive woman as *Dorrie Doormat*. When Dorrie is non-assertive, she allows other people to make her decisions for her, even though she may later resent it.

She feels helpless, powerless, inhibited, nervous, and anxious. She rarely expresses her feelings and has little self-confidence. She does best when following others and may be fearful of taking the initiative in any situation. She feels sorry for herself to the point of martyrdom, and wonders why others cannot rescue her from her plight. When a woman *only* relates to the world passively and fails to turn to others, she frequently turns to alcoholism, drugs, physical complaints, or eating disorders to escape her misery.

AGGRESSIVE

On the other hand, *Augusta Aggressive* is very expressive, to the extent that she humiliates and deprecates others. You could call her obnoxious, vicious, or egocentric. No matter what you label her, she has the same destructive effect on you; you feel devastated by an encounter with her. Her message to you is that she's okay and you definitely are not. In our society, it takes a lot of courage for a woman to be aggressive, especially since this style of behavior has been viewed as totally non-feminine. So, the price the aggressive woman pays is usually alienation from almost everybody.

INDIRECTLY AGGRESSIVE

Because of the reaction accorded to the aggressive woman and the misery experienced by the passive woman, many women develop the ability to get what they want by indirect means. In our chart, *Isabel Indirect* illustrates this type of behavior. Isabel has learned her lesson well; in order to achieve her goal she may use trickery, seduction, or manipulation. Isabel has learned that a woman is expected to use her "womanly wiles" to get what she wants. Therefore, Isabel is seen as cute and coy. However, when she is angry, she is likely to use sneaky ways to get revenge. She can be so indirect that the person with whom she is angry may never know.

ASSERTIVE

There is another way to respond to people and situations: *assertively*. In our chart, *Allison Assertive* is expressive with her feelings — without Augusta's obnoxiousness. She is able to state her views and desires directly, spontaneously, and honestly. She feels good about herself and about others too; she respects the feelings and rights of other people. Allison can evaluate a situation, choose how to act, and then act without reservation. Allison is true to herself, but she never forgets that other people have rights too. Winning or losing seem unimportant compared to the value of expressing herself and choosing for herself. She may not always achieve her goals, but the result isn't always as important to her as the actual process of asserting herself. Regardless of whether Allison has something positive or negative to say to you, she says it in such a way that you are left with your dignity intact and with good feelings about what was said.

When our four fictional female characters were first introduced in *The Assertive Woman*, they were instantly recognized. Workshop participants and readers alike identified themselves in two or more of the characters. They wanted, perhaps, to tone down their Dorrie Doormat behavior, and make way for the emerging Allison Assertive.

It is quite rare to be similar to only one of the characters, and natural to see a little of yourself in all four. It may be helpful to allocate percentages next to each character, to represent how much that approach captures your communication style. For example, your own approach might be expressed as 20 percent passive (Dorrie), 5 percent aggressive (Augusta), 35 percent indirect (Isabel), and 40 percent assertive (Allison). If you want to change those percentages, write down your goal percentage as an incentive.

Example Scenarios

How each woman responds to given situations reveals a lot about her behavior patterns. Examine these scenarios and find yours.

"WHAT'S FOR DINNER?"

Scenario: A man and a woman, each with a full-time job, live together. The woman has her share of housework and cooking, and the man has his share of the domestic chores. She returns from work one evening quite tired, and finds her mate in the study reading the paper.

Passive: Dorrie sighs as she enters the study. She felt like going out to dinner and is really too tired to cook, but doesn't say so. She puts a smile on her face and asks sweetly, "What would you like for dinner, honey?" She quietly goes off and fixes dinner, feeling all the while like a martyr. Her mother phones while she's cooking, and Dorrie complains bitterly that she has to do *all* the work.

Aggressive: Augusta moans about what a hard day she's had. She yells at her mate, "If you think I'm going to cook when I feel this rotten, you're crazy!" She threatens to leave him if he doesn't do something about the messy house and at least take her out to a nice restaurant. She calls him a lazy slob and belittles him for not caring about her feelings. He responds by offering to help, promising to take her out, or going out alone, slamming the door behind him.

Indirectly Aggressive: Isabel steps lightly into the study and asks, "What would you like to do about dinner?" She wants him to suggest going out or at least helping her cook, but he's candid and says, "I'm tired, would you mind fixing dinner tonight?" Isabel makes an attempt to look even more tired and bedraggled, hoping again that he will take the hint. He doesn't. So, she agrees to fix dinner and proceeds to the kitchen, banging pots and pans furiously, preparing something she knows he hates, and burning it besides.

Assertive: Allison finds her mate in the study and asks that they talk for a minute about plans for dinner. She tells him that she had a hard day and is feeling quite tired, and asks how he's feeling. She suggests that they either fix dinner together or go out to eat, since he said he was feeling tired too. She understands his feelings, but does not cheat herself by hiding her own. They reach a compromise: neither feels like a martyr or put down. They enjoy dinner together in a relaxed atmosphere.

"YOU'RE NOT INTERESTED IN MY WORK!"

Scenario: A husband and wife are struggling to succeed in related fields. The man complains that his wife is not interested in *his* work because she doesn't take an active and enthusiastic role in finding out more about what he does and why he does it. She isn't usually available to accompany him on business-related trips. He feels she should make a greater effort to be gracious and to entertain his work associates.

Passive: Dorrie feels guilty. She is convinced that her husband's success or failure depends on how much responsibility she takes in playing an auxiliary role in his job. She vows to find a way to please him. She minimizes her own needs regarding *her* work and its limitations and demands. To keep peace, she gives in and puts his interests first.

Aggressive: Instantly Augusta's defenses flare up. She argues with her husband, recounting instances when she has supported him and he hasn't appreciated it. Then she launches an attack about the times when she needed him, and he obviously didn't care at all. They both feel alienated, misunderstood and hurt. The problem is sure to flare up again.

Indirectly Aggressive: The last thing Isabel wants to do is take any responsibility for her husband's accusations. Even if she were guilty of sabotaging his work (typical for Isabel), she would never admit it. She tries to manipulate him by bemoaning how her work "forces" her to be less supportive of him. She is dishonest about "feeling terrible" for him and in her own sweet-but-back-stabbing way, she puts him down for being weak and unable to stand on his own "like a man." She doesn't seem to recognize she would feel different if the tables were turned and she needed his support. She feels self-righteous; he feels threatened and alone.

Assertive: Allison listens to her husband's complaints. She encourages him to express how he feels about the situation: his anger, frustration, hurt, and aloneness. Then she shares with him how she really feels about the issue. She is able to understand his need for support and recognizes the legitimacy of that need within him as well as within herself. Allison then asserts that there may be some things that each can do to be mutually supportive. She explores alternatives with him, for example, by suggesting that they spend an hour or a day at each other's place of work once in a while, that they set aside a certain time every day (perhaps after dinner) to talk together about their feelings, that together they plan some social occasions with each other's work associates. They both feel better due to Allison's assertiveness.

STAR WARS

Scenario: Mom and dad bring their two young children, ten months and three years, to the movies — the re-release of *Star Wars*. Almost from the opening frame, the three-year old pelts her parents with nonstop questions: "Who's that?" and "What is the man doing?" Meanwhile, the baby sputters and finally starts to bawl. The parents try to calm the kids, but moviegoers seated nearby are getting fed up with the noise and disruption.

Passive: Dorrie rolls her eyes and heaves a loud sigh in the general direction of the screaming child. She coughs and even tries clearing her throat, but nothing happens. These people don't notice her forlorn attempts to get them to move. Oh, well, Dorrie thinks, kids have a right to be here, too, and I'd be so embarrassed to say anything to them. Maybe they've had a hard day. I'll just sit tight and try to ignore the fuss, even though this really spoils things for me.

Aggressive: Augusta can see where this is going, and she's not about to have her favorite movie ruined by a couple of bratty kids making a scene in the row in front of her. Augusta stridently complains to those around her that "If they're too cheap to get a sitter, they could've stayed home and rented a video." When the noise continues, Augusta ups the ante: She kicks the mom's seat back and says, "What part of 'no talking in the movie' don't you understand? Either you shut them up, or I'll make sure the manager throws you out!" The family does leave, to a smattering of applause, but they call their lawyer the very next morning. They're suing the theater for harassment.

Indirect: Since the movie (and the unwanted noise) started, Isabel has been busy plotting her revenge. As she shifts in her seat, Isabel "accidentally" spills some buttered popcorn into the dad's lap; when he looks up, the "apology" Isabel offers is through clenched teeth. When the group still doesn't budge, Isabel decides to fight fire with fire, and launches into a loud conversation with her seatmate about the disgusting decline of courtesy and manners in American society today.

Assertive: Allison knows what it's like to be in a public place struggling with restless kids, and she can empathize with the parents sitting in front of her. Their hullabaloo is obliterating the movie, though, and Allison decides to speak to the parents about it. She gently taps the mom on the shoulder and says calmly, "Excuse me, the noise is making it impossible to watch the movie. I know how difficult it is with young children —— I had two of my own —— but I'd appreciate it if you would take the little one out to the lobby until she quiets down." When the movie ends (or before if her assertive request didn't succeed), Allison finds the theater manager, explains the problem, and asks that management enforce its "no children under five" policy.

A good look in the mirror is the first step toward assertiveness. Deepen your understanding of what triggers the appearance of Dorrie, Augusta, Isabel, or Allison in you. Consider your important relationships: spouse, partner, coworker, roommate, boss, children, parents. Who has the upper hand, and when? How do you resolve conflicts? Are you quick to anger, or do you stand by, afraid to make waves? As always, be aware of your body's image as well as what's on your mind.

Suggested Reading

An Unknown Woman, by Alice Koller. New York: Bantam Books, 1991.

The Mists of Avalon, by Marion Zimmer Bradley. New York: Little Brown, 1995.

Chapter 4

Becoming Assertive

One's philosophy is not best expressed in words, it is expressed in the choices one makes... In the long run, we shape our lives and we shape ourselves. The process never ends until we die. And the choices we make are ultimately our responsibility.

---- Eleanor Roosevelt

Acquiring new assertive behaviors involves becoming aware of your own attitudes, actions and reactions, and knowing which will promote your assertion and which will delay it. It also involves becoming aware of the possible consequences of choosing to be assertive.

For example, as you begin to behave more assertively, you may find that you are working against old, non-assertive behavior patterns that you learned years before. Applying some basic learning principles will help you to develop and maintain assertive behaviors as you combat old behavior patterns. Using the guidelines in this chapter will prepare the way for your continued success in becoming assertive.

Social behaviors are learned and practiced over time. You become assertive by paying attention to your attitudes as well as to specific behaviors. Whether or not the environment will support your newly-adopted behaviors is also an important consideration.

Attitudes

Knowing how you feel about yourself is the first step toward learning assertive behaviors. From childhood you may have developed attitudes that inhibit learning assertiveness. Some possibilities are listed below. Which did you grow up with?

* Women should be seen and not heard.
* I am helpless when it comes to taking action that promotes change.
* I don't like risk-taking; it scares me.
* I'd rather let somebody else be the leader. I'm a good follower.
* What other people think is more important than what I think.
* It's better to put up with things than rock the boat.
* If I ask for what I want people will think I'm selfish.
* It's better to be liked than speak up and be seen as a troublemaker.
* Girls who assert themselves are being aggressive.
* A woman who is too competent will never find a husband.

Your thoughts and attitudes alone can perpetuate non-assertive behavior. If you believe it would be *terrible* for you to behave assertively, you aren't likely to give it a try. Exploring the thoughts and attitudes that prevent you from expressing yourself can actually help you to stimulate positive new behaviors.

For example, Dorrie Doormat may think to herself:

"If I tried to assert myself in this situation, I know I'd say the wrong thing and people would think I'm stupid and unfeminine. *That would be terrible.* I'd never live through it." By imagining catastrophic consequences, Dorrie is effectively teaching herself not to be assertive. Allison would have quite a different attitude: "If I try to assert myself in this situation, I will feel better because I'm saying or doing something. By expressing my views, I know I will benefit."

Try to be aware of the imagined consequences you attach to asserting yourself. If you find you have some *attitudes* which discourage acting assertively, make a conscious effort to have those attitudes work *for* you instead of against you. Try repeating to yourself, "I will say or do something in this situation because I believe it could be effective. I will benefit from asserting myself." If you practice saying this as you begin new behaviors, it will be easier for you to progress in self-assertion.

Also, try to *visualize* yourself acting assertively and experiencing positive consequences. If you frequently see yourself failing to be assertive, imagine some situations in which you are successfully assertive. As you visualize yourself becoming more positive, your self-image will change also. The more you regard yourself as an assertive woman, the more likely you are to behave assertively.

For many women, attitudes about what is feminine prevent them from behaving assertively. Women who feel it is unfeminine or aggressive to behave assertively have two alternatives: to behave passively or to be coy and indirectly aggressive. The result of either approach is to avoid an opportunity to develop assertiveness.

Perhaps you have avoided acting independently and assertively because of the anxiety or fear involved in changing your behavior. If you consider the anxiety and pain you have felt when you acted non-assertively, you will find that assertion is a welcome alternative.

Behaviors

Learning new behaviors involves at least these four steps:
1. Description or modeling of the behavior;
2. Practicing the new behavior;
3. Reinforcing the desired behavior; and
4. Receiving accurate, rapid feedback.

As you learn assertive behaviors, an awareness of their causes (antecedents) and their results (consequences) is also important. Let's examine each of these elements in turn:

1. Description or modeling of the behavior

Throughout this book we present descriptions and illustrations of appropriate behaviors that will serve as assertive models for you. Before you begin attempting to increase your assertiveness, be sure you understand the difference between assertive and aggressive behaviors. It is also worthwhile to talk with or observe someone you consider to be an assertive person. Research has shown that learning takes place as a result of observation as well as through descriptions of the appropriate behavior.

2. Practicing the new behavior

Your first attempts at assertion should be those which will likely meet with positive consequences. Choose situations in which you are likely to experience control. If you try to tackle more difficult areas too fast, you risk negative consequences which could discourage you from asserting yourself in the future. For example, it would generally be wiser to assertively give a compliment as a beginning, rather than attempt to assertively handle someone who is manipulating you. If you proceed gradually, from initial assertions to increasingly difficult ones, you will increase your probability of success.

3. Reinforcing the desired behavior

Arrange it initially so you are likely to be rewarded, rather than punished, for your assertive behavior. As you continue to behave assertively, you will find that just the act of being assertive is in itself rewarding. We cannot stress enough that the goal of assertion is not "victory," but being able to express your needs and desires openly and honestly. Remember, the compulsion to win at all costs is the burden of the aggressive person.

4. Receiving accurate, rapid feedback

When you are practicing assertive behaviors, ask a friend to give you feedback on your behavior:

Did my assertive words match my body image?

Did I use my voice, gestures, and posture assertively?

Are there specific areas that need improvement?

Which ones?

You can also give yourself accurate feedback with the help of a mirror, or an audio or video tape recorder. Practice assertive behaviors in front of a mirror before you try it in the real situation; use an audio tape recorder to receive feedback about the tone, volume, and quality of your voice. Videotape feedback is the clearest overall measure of your effectiveness. You may be surprised, when you use these feedback tools, to discover that your self-expression is not as assertive as you had thought.

Combining a knowledge of what assertive behavior is with actually performing it and receiving reinforcement and feedback will provide you with a strong foundation you can build on. It is a good formula to follow as you develop assertive responses. Practice and preparation beforehand will make it much more likely that you will continue to behave assertively. Practice or rehearse your assertive behaviors using the exercises in this book. The more attention you give to *practicing* assertive behaviors, the more comfortable you will be in asserting yourself.

In spite of your preparation and new knowledge, you may still find it difficult to behave assertively. If you find yourself being generally non-assertive, you may benefit from the extra support and guidance that a professional counselor or therapist can provide. Changing your lifestyle is not easy. Many women have combined other resources to help them become more assertive: the help of professional therapists or facilitators, reading books, attending workshops, or enrolling in classes.

Antecedents and Consequences of Behavior

Knowing what causes or stimulates your behavior and being aware of how your behavior affects you and others are both important steps in learning new behaviors. Specifying the antecedents and the consequences of your behavior can support you in your efforts to be assertive.

Antecedents. People and situations influence you to behave in certain patterns. Identifying the ones that have led you to behave non-assertively in the past will give you direction for behaving assertively in the future.

Sharon Bower, in her book, *Learning Assertive Behavior With PALS*, has developed a comprehensive list of people and situations to use in identifying who or what may cause women to behave non-assertively. We have condensed it here. Use it as a starting point for developing your awareness of situations you can handle more assertively.

Place a check beside the items that influence you to behave non-assertively. After you have finished, review the items you have checked. You will have a list to use in guiding your progress toward more effective assertive behavior.

1. With *whom* do you feel passive or non-assertive?
_____a spouse?
_____children?
_____a relative?
_____friends?
_____an employer?
_____an employee?
_____a teacher?
_____a doctor?
_____a police officer?
_____a sales clerk?
_____waiters or waitresses?
_____an acquaintance?
_____other: _____

2. When have you felt non-assertive, especially as you
   ask for:
   ____cooperation from spouse, children, employer, employees?
   ____a loan of money or an item?
   ____a favor?
   ____a job?
   ____love and attention?
   ____directions?
   ____other: _____

3. *What* subject has caused you to behave non-assertively:
   ____sex?
   ____politics?
   ____women's rights?
   ____your accomplishments?
   ____others' accomplishments?
   ____your mistakes?
   ____others' mistakes?
   ____expressing positive feelings?
   ____expressing negative feelings?
   ____other: _____

4. *Size* of the group might be a factor in your non-assertive behavior;
   did the situation involve you and:
   ____one other familiar person?
   ____one other unfamiliar person?
   ____two or more familiar persons?
   ____two or more unfamiliar persons?
   ____a group of familiar persons?
   ____a group of unfamiliar persons?

Consequences. Your behavior has consequences; it affects other people. Women who have behaved passively for long periods of time usually acknowledge that the behavior of others affects them, but they are seldom aware of the extent to which their passive behaviors affect others. Recognizing the consequences of your behavior is an important element in learning assertive behaviors.

Assertive behavior is likely to have positive consequences. When you assert yourself, you will feel more in control of your life and less helpless and frustrated. While you remain passive, the consequences are likely to be painful for you and for others. Other people may resent you for being so dependent on them or for allowing them to make your decisions for you. They may feel burdened by your non-assertiveness.

There may also be people who have actually encouraged you to behave passively. Your mate, for example, may have reinforced your passive behavior by labeling your assertive attempts as aggressive, or by blaming you for difficulties in your relationship. In such a situation it is understandable that you would feel anxious about expressing yourself, because you have experienced such negative consequences in the past. Professional counseling or assertiveness training for you and the other family members might be recommended. If your family members are prepared and willing to try to make some changes themselves, you are all likely to benefit, physically and emotionally.

For the best results, remember to choose initial assertions that are likely to promote positive consequences. You will be less likely to be discouraged in the future. Don't attempt more difficult assertions until you have had sufficient practice and preparation, and feel comfortable with previous ones.

In summary, your attitudes and previous ways of behaving affect your new attempts to behave assertively. Planning your approach to learning of assertive behaviors will help you to experience success with few setbacks.

• Consider your thoughts and attitudes about being assertive: Which ones encourage and support an assertive image of yourself?

• Are you avoiding assertion because you fear disastrous consequences?

• Be aware of the situations and people that have influenced you to be passive in the past, and use them as reminders to be assertive in the future.

• Practice new behaviors that result in positive consequences.

• Stay *away* from people who punish your attempts to be assertive.

• Seek out people who reward your assertive attempts with positive feedback.

• Look at becoming assertive as a positive experience, instead of a negative problem-solving venture. Remember, learning to be assertive can be fun!

In the next few chapters, we'll focus on attitudes, beliefs, thoughts, and feelings: The "Inner Game of Assertiveness." In later chapters, we'll deal with the behavioral skills you'll need to express yourself.

Suggested Reading

See You At The Top, by Zig Ziglar. Gretna, Louisiana: Pelican Publishing Co., 1984.

Self-Assertion For Women, by Pamela E. Butler. San Francisco: Harper & Row, Publishers, 1992.

Chapter 5

The Inner Game of Assertiveness

...I am a fairly inexperienced, often naive young woman, who is not always certain of what is right and wrong, what's worth pursuing in life, or even what I myself want out of life.... Knowledge has always come quickly and easily for me, whereas wisdom has been a difficult thing for me to put my finger on and be sure that's where it lay.

---- A twenty-four-year-old college student

In the 1970s, world-class athletes discovered how to use visualization and imagery training to increase their levels of peak performance. The visualization process was very effective, and today, athletes continue to use and refine imagery techniques. They learn how to relax instead of tensing up before a game or event, to stop labeling themselves as "stupid" or "weak," and to actually "see" themselves winning. They imagine vivid scenarios in which they play superbly, using their inner intelligence to play the "inner game." Athletes have learned to create the emotional experience of winning as if it were already happening, all before they begin to compete!

For some, playing the inner game made playing the outer game as natural and automatic as breathing, and their concentration, confidence and performance improved tremendously. Olympic decathlon champion Bruce Jenner understands the process well, and explains how to develop our inner game in his book, *Find the Champion Within*.

The Inner Game of Assertiveness

If the inner game can work so well in athletics, it is worth exploring its usefulness in other challenging areas of our lives. The concept of inner wisdom is an old one. Some of us already play an inner game as a result of religious education or metaphysical pursuits, but many people do not exercise their inner wisdom.

The inner game of assertiveness places importance on the spirit in which an assertive action is taken. To play the inner game, one trusts her own intuition or inner wisdom, evaluating herself spontaneously in relationship to her situation, then applying assertive skills accordingly. The inner game of assertiveness is a flowing, constant interaction between thoughts and behavior, between inner wisdom and assertive action.

Let's look at an example of how the inner game can be applied in everyday life.

"NOBODY WANTS TO LISTEN TO ME"

Dorinda has recently completed a time management seminar that has inspired her to get her life in order. She buys a daily planner book and spends the weekend reorganizing herself. While doing so, she sees some applications that would be beneficial at the office where she is a secretary. On Monday morning she goes into the office filled with enthusiasm to get everybody else organized, from the boss to her co-workers. She greets everyone with instant enthusiasm and pelts them with creative ideas on how to increase productivity.

When people respond with indifference, agitation or resistance, Dorinda realizes that her assertions have fallen on deaf ears.

This is an opportunity for Dorinda to play the inner game. She can acknowledge that she may have caught people off guard, that her timing was inappropriate. At a quiet time, perhaps her morning coffee break, she allows herself to calm down and really think about what she wants to accomplish with her boss and co-workers. She realizes that she wants to encourage receptivity in them and a spirit of cooperation. As she quietly meditates on this, she understands that she antagonized people by attempting to force *her* ideas onto them. Now she recognizes that it would be better to approach them in the spirit of teamwork, at a time when they will be receptive.

She finally decides to summarize of the most innovative and practical ideas she learned in her seminar. She makes arrangements with her boss to distribute copies at the next staff meeting as a contribution to all. She can then invite comments, additional ideas and feedback. Such give and take opens the possibility for eventual implementation of the best ideas. However, she is now clear that others are not approving or rejecting her personally. With her ego out of the way, everyone is able to embrace some of the new ideas more easily. Dorinda's assertive action based on her inner wisdom produces winning results.

Finding Inner Wisdom and Using It

When life is calm and clear, it is easy to make time to be centered and let inner wisdom be your guide. The challenge is much greater in the throes of real life dramas. Yet, inner wisdom evolves out of trusting yourself in spite of what's happening around you. It is a product of confronting such internal barriers as runaway emotions or negative, self-defeating thoughts.

"HOW COULD YOU DO THIS!"

Today is Sarah's mother's birthday --- a joyous occasion, or so she thought. An intimate gathering of close family and friends is to meet at her parents' home for a special tribute dinner party. Sarah dresses up for the celebration and is looking forward to a good time. Her mother hasn't been feeling well lately but Sarah is sure this party will cheer her up.

When Sarah arrives she finds her father in an anxious state. Her mother is in bed "sick." Actually Sarah's mother is an alcoholic, who on occasion drinks herself into oblivion. Everyone has felt helpless at these times but has chosen to ignore the problem and make excuses. But there is no excuse for this. The other guests will arrive soon. What to do?

In the midst of other people's disapproval, hysteria and fear, Sarah is barraged by her own defenses as well: "How could your own mother do this to *you* on her birthday?! What will people think now? You ought to be darn good and mad! Why don't you just leave this mess!" This is an opportune time for Sarah to activate her inner wisdom and play the inner game of assertiveness.

Because of the surrounding chaos, Sarah doesn't have the leisure to go off and ponder the situation peacefully. She is forced by circumstances to act more quickly and spontaneously. This she can do easily if she has been practicing the inner game consciously and consistently already. In a matter of seconds she can take a few deep breaths, shut out the noise, and allow her inner wisdom to speak to her.

As she calms herself and lets go of her judgments about what an awful thing her mother has done, she understands that her mother has chosen *the perfect time* to reach out for help. What a smart idea! Within a short time Sarah has let go of her reactions and has begun to *take positive action*. She assertively reassures her father and enlists the assistance of the less anxious guests to make arrangements for her mother's physical and medical needs. She extends a loving attitude to her mother, who knows the difference even in her state of oblivion. After the immediate concerns are handled, Sarah uses this opportunity while all are gathered to address her mother's alcoholism openly. She enlists the support of the others to deal with this family problem together in a more direct and assertive way.

To activate inner wisdom during times of pain or pressure, you must *slow down*. Take time to be alone, take a walk, meditate, listen to calming music and breathe deeply and slowly. You may even practice deep muscle relaxation as discussed in Chapter 11. If you ease the pressure to find an immediate answer to your current challenge, an answer will come from your inner wisdom. The genius of it may even surprise you. And the fact that it is *your* answer and not someone else's opinion will delight you.

What is the price of turning your back on your inner wisdom? Fear and uncertainty. If you are not willing to trust yourself, other people and events will determine the direction of *your* life. Your assertions will hit and miss, because they will be buffeted about by others' ever-changing opinions and well-meaning advice. Perhaps others can provide appropriate answers for you from time to time. However, there is no person or self-help book that knows your heart better than you do!

If you can answer the following questions with a "yes" ---- even a nervous "yes" ---- you are ready to find your inner wisdom and begin a new process of assertion. You are ready to play the inner game!

* Am I willing to listen to my heart, follow my passion, activate my inner wisdom even if it means giving up what is secure and familiar?
* Am I willing to lose the approval of others and risk rejection if it means being true to myself and self-respecting?
* Am I willing to give up my addiction to what I think I *should* feel, do, or have, in exchange for being who I am?
* Am I willing to go through any awkwardness and make mistakes as I'm learning to tune into my inner self?
* Am I willing to choose assertions out of the spirit within me, rather than choosing assertions that appear "right" or "perfect?"

* Am I willing and ready to trust myself? Do I believe that I'm worth it?

Keeping Track of Inner Wisdom

Today it is not so important to conform to rigid standards as it is to acknowledge and appreciate our uniqueness. We are waking up to the passion and promise of our own energy, intuition and creativity.

We need new ways to keep track of where we're going; it's no longer enough to measure ourselves by competing with someone else. Although we still enjoy matching wits in intellectual games, keeping score in athletics, and competing in business, we are also making progress in business, science, medicine and even world affairs through the integration of intuition and logic.

On a more personal level, we can accelerate our use of inner wisdom and ability to play the inner game through some special learning tools.

One of the most effective ways to keep track of your personal progress is to keep a journal, a blank book in which you record ---- on a daily or less frequent basis ---- your innermost thoughts, feelings, questions, even dreams. You can include conversations you've had with yourself or others. It is personal, private and confidential; keep it in a safe place so you'll feel secure in being open and vulnerable with what is written. Yes, it does sound a lot like what we used to call a "diary." The major difference is that now you'll be more systematic and purposeful about your own growth and change. Periodically read through earlier entries and look for patterns, blind spots and progress from which your inner wisdom can be strengthened.

Another possibility to consider, especially if you are not inclined to write, is to tape record your journal entries. Listening to your own voice and its many moods and changes can be a powerful learning experience. Besides developing and tracking your inner wisdom, these tools can assist you in having compassion for yourself, letting go of the old, and forgiving yourself for past mistakes.

Susan L. Harris, California entrepreneur and creator of "The Glass Ceiling... SHATTER IT!™" symbolic jewelry, wrote the following poem as she left her corporate career and listened to her inner wisdom:

The Pause Button*

As I pause
for station identification
(or Susan identification, if you will...)
I realize that I have been remotely controlled
all these years
Reacting automatically to my buttons being pushed
by family, friends, corporations —
Never pausing long enough
from each season's new competitive line-up
to question the desirability of the programming.
For years the show was a tremendous success:
>High ratings,
>Financial rewards,
>Recognition...

Until one day the screen blurred,
>filled with static and interference,
>became completely out of focus,

and the screen went blank.
Now
As I try to refocus, reprogram,
and redirect the show
I find I am not yet ready
to explore the multitude of channels
until I am more finely tuned.
Although this inaction
frustrates my sponsors and networks,
it does not, in any way,
diminish my appreciation for their support.
Instead
I am more comfortable pressing the pause button
Waiting for reception to become clearer
Finally trusting that my internal antenna,
whose signal is steadily growing stronger,
will lead the way
As long as I stay still enough to hear.

---

* Used with permission from Susan L. Harris ©1990.

Developing Assertive Attitudes

Assertiveness is only one tool that you may choose to employ to better your life. It is not the answer to every question; it is not the solution to every problem. As you explore your attitudes and deepen your awareness, you will be able to identify the ways in which assertiveness can be valuable to you personally. You can accelerate your own "consciousness raising" with our "consciousness razors." The concept of consciousness raising certainly has merit; it is the process of increasing awareness and heightening perceptions. Yet we especially like the pun on the word "razor," because it implies that each razor has a sharp edge to help you cut through some attitudes that may inhibit your assertiveness.

Using Consciousness Razors

Following is a list of razors. Try to answer each item as honestly as possible. After responding to each item, review your thoughts carefully, and write your comments in your journal.

* Have you ever felt different from other women?
* Have you felt competitive with other women?
* Were you treated differently from your brother(s) or other male relatives as you were growing up? How?
* Have you ever felt pressured into having sex?
* Have you ever pressured yourself into having sex?
* Have you ever lied about orgasm?
* Have you ever felt like a sex object?
* Do you ever feel invisible?
* Do you often feel insignificant?
* What was your relationship to your parents?
* What was your parents' relationship to you?
* How was your education affected by your being female?
* How was your interest in sports affected by your being female?
* How was your career choice affected by your being female?
* How do you feel about getting old?
* How do (did) you feel about your mother's aging?
* What do you fear most about aging?
* What goal have you wanted most to achieve in your life?
* What, if anything, has stopped you from achieving this goal?
* Do you see yourself operating in a dependent and/or in an independent way? How?

* How do you relate to authority figures? (Clergy, doctor, police...)
* Have you ever felt powerful?
* How do you feel about your body?
* Have you ever punished yourself? When? How?
* Have you ever forbidden yourself a pleasure, a meal, or some other gratification?
* Have you ever pinched or slapped yourself?
* Do you often feel a sense of aloneness or loneliness?
* Do you have some attitudes that could inhibit your being more assertive?
* What are they?
* Which affect you the most?
* Which affect you the least?

As you review your comments on the consciousness razors, look for:

• Patterns or habits that seem to repeat themselves in your life.

• Rationalizations about why you do or don't do something.

Explore your feelings in depth, trying to avoid an intellectual exercise in pursuit of the "right" answer. The goal of consciousness raising is to know yourself better and to accept who you are as well as to undertake the changes that you decide to make.

Choosing Your Own Labels

Developing an assertive attitude is an important part of becoming an assertive woman. If your attitudes and feelings about being assertive are positive and supportive, you can *reward* your assertive behavior. However, if you feel you are being "impolite," "bossy," or "bitchy" when you assert yourself, you can inhibit your assertive behavior and seriously weaken your assertive attitude. You can strengthen or minimize your assertive skills by the *labels* you place on them.

Do the labels *you* apply to your assertive behavior encourage or prevent you from being assertive? Use *positive* self-labels to support and encourage your assertive behavior. ("I'm really being assertive ---- I love it!"). *Negative* self-labels can only serve to inhibit and prevent your assertiveness. ("What a bitch I am!")

Other people can mislabel your assertive behavior also. Because women have been expected to behave passively for so long, becoming an assertive woman seems to be an extreme contrast. Other people's expectations of how you behave are being thwarted if you have been consistently passive with them, and are now being assertive. They will be quick to label your behavior as aggressive in an attempt to inhibit it, fearing they may have to change, too. This is particularly true for people close to you (family members, other relatives, close friends, employers) who have in some way benefited from your passivity (see Chapter 7, "Compassion Can Be A Trap"). On the other hand, if you have been consistently aggressive in your interactions with others, moving to a more assertive way of relating will usually be encouraged, and given positive labels by those around you.

Be aware of the negative self-labels you attach to your assertive behavior, and work toward replacing those labels with more positive ones. If you do this, other people can follow your example and work at changing their labels also. Use the following exercise to see how *you* label your assertive behavior by comparing your responses with the responses of our four women, Dorrie Doormat, Augusta Aggressive, Isabel Indirect, and Allison Assertive. Each of these situations were handled assertively, but it is the label each woman has attached to the assertive behavior that varies here. How would you label each assertion?

"THANKS, BUT NO THANKS..."

You have been telephoned by a solicitor who is trying to sell you a magazine subscription. You say you aren't interested in receiving the magazine and end the conversation. Do you think to yourself:

Dorrie Doormat: "I really didn't *want* the magazine, but wasn't I impolite and irritable to say so? The next time I'm asked to subscribe, I'll be more polite and do it."

Isabel Indirect: "Well, I certainly was easy on him! I should have said yes, and then refused to pay the subscription to teach them a lesson about bothering me."

Augusta Aggressive: "I wish I'd given that solicitor a piece of my mind! What an insolent person! The next time that happens I won't be so mild-mannered and meek."

Allison Assertive: "I was really assertive with that solicitor. I feel good about being honest and direct."

"GET READY FOR DINNER"

Your children are playing outside and you want them to come in for dinner. You go outside and tell them to come in now. They protest that it's not that late and couldn't they play for a while longer? You firmly tell them again to come in, and they do. Do you think to yourself:

Dorrie Doormat: "I'm glad they came in, but wasn't I nagging and bossy? I don't want to nag, so I think in the future I'll ask once, and if they don't come in, I'll just try to keep dinner warm."

Isabel Indirect: "I'm sure they would have come in sooner if I'd not been so polite. Instead of asking twice, I should have just said okay and waited until dinner was burned for them to come in. Then they'd feel bad."

Augusta Aggressive: "Was I quiet and passive! What a softie! Next time I'll teach those kids who's boss around here. I'll really give them a lecture!"

Allison Assertive: "I'm glad they came in when I asked them to. I'm really being assertive and honest with them."

"YOU'RE LATE!"

You are scheduled to meet a friend for an important meeting. She is an hour late when she arrives. You tell her that you are upset because she is so late, and you would have liked more time to spend with her. She acknowledges your feelings and says she will try to be on time in the future. Do you think to yourself:

Dorrie Doormat: "I'm really pleased that she will make an effort to be on time in the future, but wasn't I awfully aggressive and mean to say anything about it? I hate being so aggressive, so I'll stop demanding things and just hope they work out from now on."

Isabel Indirect: "She might be on time in the future, but I shouldn't have said anything about it today. It's so embarrassing to have to go out of my way to say something about it. I should just be late next time and see how *she* feels."

Augusta Aggressive: "I sure let her off easy. What an inconsiderate woman to be late! I should have really told her off."

Allison Assertive: "I'm really glad that our meeting will be on time in the future, and I'm pleased that I was assertive and mentioned it today. I was really honest and spontaneous, and I like it."

If Dorrie's responses sound all too familiar to you, you have been mislabeling assertive behavior as aggressive, bitchy, impolite, nagging, bossy. You are also inhibiting your own assertive behavior by attaching an inappropriate, undesirable label to it. Remember that *aggressive* behavior such as Augusta's could be labeled "nagging," "bossy," or "bitchy" ---- *not* assertive behavior.

If your labels are more like Isabel's, you are looking for revenge or trying to elicit guilt rather than rewarding your assertive behavior. You are mislabeling your assertive behavior as too easy, too direct, or embarrassing. If Augusta's labels resemble yours, you are mislabeling your appropriate assertive behavior as weak, passive or meek. The assertive woman, Allison, correctly identifies her assertive behavior as direct, spontaneous, and honest. She rewards her own assertiveness accordingly.

Attach appropriate labels to your assertive behavior, and make a conscious effort to tell yourself you've been assertive. By rewarding yourself whenever you are assertive, you'll support your own progress toward becoming an assertive woman.

Suggested Reading

Finding the Champion Within, by Bruce Jenner and Mark Seal. New York: Simon & Schuster, 1997.

Goddesses in Everywoman: A New Psychology of Women, by Jean Shinoda Bolen, M.D. New York: HarperCollins, 1985.

If: Questions for the Game of Life, by Evelyn McFarlane and James Saywell. New York: Villard Books, 1996.

Women Who Run With the Wolves, by Clarissa Pinkola Estes, Ph.D. New York: Ballantine Books, 1992.

Chapter 6

Obstacles On The Inner Journey

Dear Stanlee and Nancy,

I've dressed for success, had my colors done, new make-up, hair-style ---- in short, a complete overhaul. I've eliminated sissy words from my vocabulary and replaced them with power phrases. I've attended seminars, absorbed the latest books on self-improvement, joined the right organizations and professional groups, lived through divorce and am financially independent. I seem to have done it all and have it all. But, with accomplishing this and more, why do I still doubt myself? What does it take to honestly believe I'm an assertive woman in my guts?

---- Forty-one years old,
vice president for marketing of a large corporation.

Looking like an assertive woman can be accomplished a lot faster than feeling like one. For years women have been inundated with advice about how to become today's new woman. Quick-fix techniques, images and accouterments have been heavily promoted, with the hope they would immediately and permanently transform the women who used them.

Instead, there are lots of women today who look assertive, but who don't believe they *are* assertive. They have adopted styles and behaviors recommended by experts, spouses, friends, coworkers, or society in general. In many instances they have paid a high price for these changes ---- time, energy and money which has left them far short of real, deep-down transformation.

Some women have resigned themselves to a perpetual self-improvement campaign as if it were a life sentence. Some, weary of pursuing a new assertive woman identity, reverted to more traditional or less demanding roles. Others ride a merry-go-round of confusion, chasing quick fixes of enlightenment, followed by periods of hopelessness and lethargy. And still others cautiously guard their assertive woman image ---- a precarious balance of outward appearances ---- like a trophy that might be snatched away at any moment.

The need to conform to what others expect has been a major preoccupation for many women. It is no surprise many women feel like impostors: they know that their insides don't match their outsides. They feel cheated and tired, but they are afraid to admit it. The fear of being found out keeps their defenses high.

To be an assertive woman, and not just look like one, requires an important shift toward the discovery of and respect for one's inner self. A good beginning is to learn to let go of the drive to win another's approval.

The Assertive Woman: Fashioned from Within

The next step toward becoming an assertive woman presents obstacles of a different nature. A new selection of how-to books, seminar workshops, and self-help manuals describes these pitfalls. Just when we thought we might relax a little and coast along on some of our mini-triumphs, we're barraged with a whole new wave of syndromes, complexes and situations to overcome. The challenges seem endless. And, there are new lists of what to *do* and what you need to *have* to survive.

The assertive woman is challenged to be a unique individual in her relationships with herself, others and her career. Again she looks not for answers about what to *do* or what to *have* but who she wants to *be*. Her answers come from within.

Obstacles to the Inner Journey

Today, we think of women in the space program as a regular fact of life. Dr. Shannon Lucid's six-month journey in 1996 aboard the Russian Mir space station was highly praised, but didn't really surprise us. It wasn't that long ago that women had to fight hard for acceptance, however. During a 1985 Women in Management Conference, Sally Ride, America's first female astronaut was asked by someone in the audience, "Did you get your brains from your father?" She replied, "I must have, because my mother still has hers!" Her speech was warm, humorous and powerful. From the way she spoke about her life as a woman and an astronaut, it was apparent to all that Sally was centered from within.

Barriers to the inner process generally fall into three categories: (1) cognitive or thought barriers; (2) emotional addictions; and (3) social barriers. Any or all of these can sabotage the sincerest efforts to be assertive.

Thought barriers often come to us in the guise of self-stereotyping or negative self-labeling. A constant voice in the back of your head can be heard at any time you choose to listen. We call her "Ms. Protecto." Her chatter provides you with a perpetual stream of judgements, positive and negative. Ms. Protecto's negative comments can be definite barriers. She thinks she's protecting you from getting hurt or other dangers. Actually she's preventing you from meeting the assertive woman inside who needs and wants to grow, take calculated risks, and pursue the adventure and rewards of being assertive. Do you recognize any of these thought barriers from your Ms. Protecto?

"This will never work.... I can't.... I'll never be able to change.... I'll wait and see, wait and see, on and on.... It's not right to do what *I* want to do.... Nobody cares anyway.... I'm not thin enough (good enough, smart enough).... What if I fail? I'm rejected? She/he gets angry?.... This is too much work.... The world will never change anyway.... There's no such thing as inner wisdom, especially inside *me!*... If you can't beat 'em, join 'em.... Somebody needs to help me because I can't do it alone.... This is ridiculous, just somebody else's idea.... I can't think.... What's the use anyway?... It's just bad Karma.... My childhood was miserable.... I'm being punished.... It's against my faith.... I don't know."

Emotional addictions can be stubborn. Not only do we manufacture these emotions ourselves, their fires are fueled by the latest fads. During the 70s, it was OK to plumb the depths of anger and sexuality. It was not in vogue to feel or express jealousy, envy, shyness, depression, guilt or regret. Instead, the emphasis was on selfishness and revenge: men and society were held responsible for the repression of female anger and sexuality. It the first edition of *The Assertive Woman* in 1975, we attempted to shift women's awareness from "what have they done to me?" to "what am I continuing to do to myself?"

An assertive woman seeks to take responsibility for herself, including anger and her sexuality. She knows she has choices about the intensity of her feelings and the way in which she expresses them.

Much has been said and done to demystify anger and sexuality, but addiction to an emotional merry-go-round is still alive. It has taken on new forms which are just as oppressive as the old. The message is the same: somebody else knows more about how I'm supposed to feel and not feel than I do!

For example, today's designer emotions include stress, burnout, and guilt about not doing it all or having it all. Absorbed as we are in trying to fix the symptoms of alcoholism, drug addiction, eating disorders and disappointments in relationships, we don't take the time to look inward.

Obsessions and emotional addictions act as barriers to our inner selves and to assertion. Assertiveness requires a commitment to begin an inner search for what is personal. We may not always know what we feel or have a designer name for it; it may not be in vogue, especially if others label it as selfish or irrelevant. The woman who is growing in assertiveness knows and trusts that her inner process will provide her with the necessary sensitivity and clarity to be an assertive woman from the inside out.

Ten Commandments for the Inner Journey

The following commandments are helpful in steering clear of the barriers to our inner journey. You may wish to put together your own list of reminders; we suggest 3" x 5" index cards to carry with you or post in clear view.

- Create quiet time.
- Risk vulnerability.
- Open to inner wisdom.
- Trust answers from within.
- Learn to laugh at Ms. Protecto.
- Let go of emotional addictions.
- Look for and develop self-approval.
- Live without negative self labels.
- Focus on *being* ---- not doing and having.
- Be responsible for creating choices.

In the following chapter, we'll take a look at another barrier to assertiveness ---- one so pervasive that it deserves a name and space all its own: The Compassion Trap.

Suggested Reading

The Cinderella Complex, by Collette Dowling. New York: Simon & Schuster, 1990.

Lives Without Balance: When You're Giving Everything You've Got and Still Not Getting What You Hoped For, by Steven Carter & Julia Sokol. New York: Villard Books, 1991.

MidLife Woman, a newsletter, published bi-monthly by MidLife Women's Network. Minneapolis, MN (612) 925-0020.

What to Say When You Talk to Yourself, by Shad Helmstetter. Scottsdale, Arizona: Grindle Press, 1986.

Chapter 7

Compassion Can Be A Trap

Show me a woman who doesn't feel guilty and I'll show you a man.

---- Erica Jong

One particularly powerful attitude that stops women in their tracks is "The Compassion Trap." In a 1971 article, Margaret Adams defined the Compassion Trap as exclusive to women who feel that they exist to serve others, and who believe they must provide tenderness and compassion to all at all times. Recognizing when and how the Compassion Trap affects *you* is an important part of developing an assertive attitude.

Years ago, it was up to Dorrie to "keep the family together" through self-sacrifice and compromise. The man of the house endured hassles outside the home, at work. Overall, the totally compassionate woman benefited society by making things comfortable, so that men could tend to the "more important concerns" of work, business, science, or politics. Now, many women still tend to cluster in the helping professions (social work, nursing, teaching, domestic services), where they extend their caretaking roles. However, many a Dorrie becomes frustrated and confused as she tries to honor her own individual preferences. She is torn between expressing herself directly ---- and thus reaping firsthand rewards ---- and supporting others, and receiving vicarious pleasure from their accomplishments.

The Compassion Trap means that a woman expresses herself chiefly through meeting others' needs, it frequently prevents women from being assertive. Climbing out of the Compassion Trap does not mean that, like Augusta, you must close yourself off from others' feelings. Instead, it means valuing your *own* feelings and treating them with the same care that you give to others, as Allison does.

Generally, there are six areas in which Dorrie, Augusta, or Isabel may find herself trapped by compassion:

1. She may see herself as a protector, as a mother who is afraid to act on her own behalf for fear that her children will suffer.

2. A single woman may give up a career to take care of her aging or sick relatives.

3. A woman may be reluctant to leave an unsatisfactory job for fear that her clients will suffer in the short run, even though she may benefit in the long run.

4. When no one else is concerned about a problem, a woman may enjoy being the one who has special understanding or compassion.

5. When a crisis arises, a woman may push aside a creative project to give her full attention to the crisis; she feels indispensable.

6. A woman may not take action even though she is a victim of the beginning stages of domestic abuse.

Some profiles will illustrate the chief variations of the Compassion Trap:

"I'M SURE HE WILL CHANGE"

Scenario: A woman has been married for five years, has no children and no income of her own. Her husband is extremely possessive and controlling and expects her to be at home most of the time. He forbids her to see her friends and verbally puts her down.

Passive: Dorrie tells herself that if she were a better wife, her husband would treat her better. She thinks that he's just under a lot of stress, and that things will eventually improve. She never talks back, and she believes him when he tells her she's worthless. She feels isolated, but she's afraid to make waves. She continually tries to please him.

Indirectly Aggressive: Isabel feels as if she's drowning in the marriage, but feels helpless to reach for a lifeline. Caught in the Compassion Trap, she wants to resolve her husband's emotional problems. As the abuse continues, however, she withdraws more and more, until she barely speaks to him when he comes home at night. She refuses to have sex with him, even though she knows her refusal will only make him angrier. She daydreams about leaving him, but never does.

Aggressive: Augusta is angry all the time, but doesn't have the inner will or resources to handle the situation. She feels beaten down and worthless, but can't communicate her feelings. Instead, she tries to put him down too, and fights with him every evening.

Assertive: Allison takes stock of the situation and realizes that this is her husband's emotional problem, not hers. She understands that she is in a very destructive relationship, and that she must make some changes. Although she still loves her husband and cares about his needs, she knows that she must care about her own needs too. She reaches out to others for support and help. When she feels strong enough, she discusses her unhappiness with her husband, tells him that she will not accept the abuse any longer and explains the consequences if the abuse continues.

It can be very difficult to change an abusive relationship. Because the victim is often isolated by the abuser, she has no support system. She is on her own, and her feelings of low self-esteem often lead to inappropriate and ineffective actions. It's not easy to be assertive in this situation, but it's the only way to end the abuse. Remember that to be assertive is to make choices in your own best interests. A very assertive way to deal with abuse is to *pack up and leave,* seeking help from family, friends, a counselor or a shelter. (See "When the Going Gets Tough" at the end of this chapter.)

"I FELT SORRY FOR HIM"

Scenario: A seventeen year old girl and her boyfriend are alone at a very "romantic" place. They have been getting closer and closer to sexual intercourse, but have always stopped just before. Tonight, he has decided to "go all the way."

Aggressive: Augusta, caught in the Compassion Trap, feels an attack is the best way to avoid a confrontation. She accuses her boyfriend of being a sex maniac, and only having "one thing on his mind all of the time." She feels it unnecessary to listen to him; her philosophy is "a good offense is the best defense." She prevents him from expressing his feelings, and continues to overreact. For Augusta, it is embarrassing to think that she could be caught in a weak moment, so she uses her aggressiveness to mask her indecision. Augusta cannot believe that expressing her feelings in an assertive way will have any impact, and she feels that the only way she can get her point across is to come on strong.

Passive: Dorrie listens intently as her boyfriend recounts the times when he felt so frustrated after being with her that he couldn't sleep all night. Dorrie feels guilty as he describes the pain he felt by not being able to ejaculate so many times in a row, night after night. She's far too embarrassed to ask him if he ever thought of masturbating to relieve the pressure. Instead, Dorrie is swept up in his intense feelings, and forgets about her own desire not to have sex. She gives in because she feels she can no longer allow him to "suffer," and she is secretly fearful that if she refuses, she'll lose him and maybe nobody else will want her.

Indirect: Isabel, like Dorrie, is not immune to the Compassion Trap. She feels sorry for her boyfriend, but she tries to mask her compassion and her panic by making excuses. Isabel lies about having her period and says intercourse would be "messy and not much fun." If this excuse does not work, she will add that she has a headache or is too tired. Isabel may even pretend to want him passionately while she makes up another story about having to get home early, or say she has promised her parents or her best friend that she would not have sex. Isabel fears that her boyfriend will not accept the truth, but she is convinced he will accept excuses!

Assertive: Allison listens to her boyfriend's feelings and complaints. She acknowledges how miserable he is feeling. She says, however, that she does not want to have intercourse. When he accuses her of being unfair and leading him on, she again repeats that it is very important to her at this time not to have sex, that she respects his feelings, and that perhaps they need to talk about alternatives such as masturbation, avoiding heavy make-out sessions, or not seeing each other. She expresses her concern for her own feelings without feeling guilty or compelled to take care of his needs. She feels confident that, if he decides not to see her anymore, she can find someone willing to respect her wishes.

Allison may refuse to go along with what her boyfriend wants for reasons of her own. She may be very concerned about the dangers of HIV or other diseases, *or* she may hold a religious belief about the importance of remaining a virgin until she marries. Or perhaps she feels that the relationship is not ready for sex. Or, Allison may be refusing her boyfriend's request because she has a health problem that may make intercourse painful for her. Whatever her reason, Allison offers it without making excuses.

From this scenario alone, we hope it is clear that it does not require a special background or unique personality type to become an Assertive

Allison. Everyone can be assertive in their own personal ways, and within the contexts of their own unique life situations.

"THEY NEED ME — THE POOR THINGS"

Scenario: A skilled, experienced nurse works for a large city hospital. Her salary is below average and the working conditions poor. Her income is not vital to the family's welfare; her husband earns a good salary. She works primarily because she loves nursing. However, she is confronted with a disorganized hospital administration, understaffing, inadequate supplies, and low morale among the nursing staff. A union organizer is trying to unite the nurses to take a stand and, if necessary, to strike for better conditions.

Passive: The Compassion Trap tells Dorrie that she and the other nurses would only be selfish to engage in hard-nosed negotiations that may lead to a strike. After all, who would see to it that Ms. Jones down the hall really swallowed her medication instead of hiding it under her tongue? Dorrie decides to put up with the poor conditions for the sake of her patients. She's frightened of confrontations and believes that a good nurse has to think of others first, keep peace and keep smiling.

Indirectly Aggressive: Isabel feels helpless when she's caught in the Compassion Trap. She is sorry for her patients, herself, and the other nurses. However, her inability to directly express her frustration leads her to find fault with other nurses, neglect her patients, and to develop a "who cares?" attitude.

Aggressive: Augusta, stuck in the Compassion Trap, is unable to communicate her concern. Instead she gives the impression that she is just an "angry bitch." As usual, she overreacts by making hostile demands and threats. She goes to the right people at the top, but she says the wrong things. The net result is that she widens the gap of misunderstanding.

Assertive: Like Augusta, Allison believes in the value of action. She is concerned about her patients' welfare, but she chooses to risk a possible strike to obtain better conditions for all in the long run. She is confident that the nurses, if united, can make a substantial impact to improve the hospital. Allison puts her compassion to good use and doesn't allow her energies to dissipate in a flurry of worry. She expresses her concern to the other nurses and urges them to organize and to take a strong, but fair, stand.

Allison asks: are we *really* helping other people so much by always pampering them and taking care of things that cause them discomfort? What price do *we* pay as individuals when our giving and compassion is done at the expense of our own happiness? What price does the *receiver* of our compassion pay when we have felt obligated and resentful? Just as much or more can be accomplished if we allow others to be assertive and take responsibility for themselves.

The Compassion Trap Quiz

Gauge the extent to which you are stuck in the Compassion Trap by taking our quiz below. Answer each question *honestly*. If you have not personally experienced some situations, choose the response that comes closest to the way you think you would respond. After you have finished, turn the page and add up your score. The corresponding key will help you to determine how "trapped" you really are.

1. You have been seeing a man socially for several weeks, but you are beginning to feel bored and disinterested. He likes you very much and would like to see you more often. Do you:

a. tell him you'd prefer not to see him, feeling you've been honest with yourself?

b. feel a sudden attack of the flu coming on?

c. continue to be the object of his affections, because leaving would really hurt his ego?

d. tell him that he bores you to tears, and that even if you were both marooned on a desert island, you would camp out on the opposite shore?

2. You invited a friend who lives out of the state to spend her/his two week vacation with you at your home. It is now one month later, and your friend shows no intention of leaving, or reimbursing you for food and telephone bills. You would like your friend to leave. Do you:

a. not mention anything about your expenses or feelings, because you don't want to damage the friendship?

b. leave a note saying that you're terribly sorry, but your mother has decided to live with you and you'll need the room?

c. tell your friend that you really value your friendship, that the extended visit is putting a strain on it, and ask that your friend make plans to leave?

d. put all of your friend's belongings out on the doorstep with a note: "Don't call me; I'll call you"?

3. You are enjoying one of your rare visits to San Francisco, and you are staying with your brother and sister-in-law. One of your favorite things to do in that city is to sample the fine restaurants. Your brother and sister-in-law are terrible cooks, but they insist on "treating" you by cooking for you themselves. You would much prefer going out to eat. Do you:

a. decide to have dinner at your brother and sister-in-law's home because you don't want to disappoint them by refusing their offer?

b. tell them that you appreciate their thoughtfulness, and explain that one of the reasons you come to San Francisco is to enjoy the restaurants, suggesting that all of you go out to eat instead?

c. loudly tell them that you're not there for *their* food?

d. call and claim that you are unavoidably detained, and tell them not to wait dinner for you — then sneak out and eat by yourself?

4. You are working on a project that is very important to you. Some friends drop by unexpectedly. You'd really like to continue working. Do you:

a. shelve your project, prepare hors d'oeuvres, and apologize for your cluttered living room?

b. loudly berate your friends for not having called first?

c. explain that you're in the middle of an important project and arrange to see them at a mutually convenient time?

d. ignore your friends and continue working on your project while they are there, hoping they'll get the message?

5. Your ten-year-old daughter customarily walks to school, but today she wants you to drive her. You have driven her on rainy days, but it is gorgeous today. She continues to ask you to drive, adding, "Besides, everyone else's mothers drive them." Do you:

a. tell your daughter she can walk to school as usual?

b. begin by telling your daughter that you won't drive her to school but after a short time you give in, feeling guilty that you hesitated?

c. reply "Oh, okay, I'll drive you," thinking of all the other children whose mothers faithfully drive them, and feeling like a neglectful mother if you don't drive your daughter to school?

d. threaten to call the truant officer and report on your daughter if she doesn't leave for school immediately?

KEY

1. a) An assertive choice. (3)
   b) Honesty is the best policy here. (0)
   c) Don't forget *your* feelings. (0)
   d) Don't forget *his* feelings. (0)

2. a) You'll feel resentful later. You're trapped. (0)
   b) This may get her/him out, but how do you feel about trapping yourself with *that* one? (1)
   c) Right. This will also get her/him out, and leave you with your self-respect. (3)
   d) This will get your friend out of your life, also. (0)

3. a) This Compassion Trap will result in your disappointment and indigestion. (0)
   b) The assertive thing to do. (3)
   c) Better look for a hotel room --- your brother and sister-in-law won't want to have you as a guest for some time. (0)
   d) You'll soon run out of excuses. Then what? (0)

4. a) The Compassion Trap. (0)
   b) Only if you *never* want to see them again. (0)
   c) Ain't it the truth? (3)
   d) You're wasting time; it may take hours for them to get the hint! (0)

5. a) You've got it! (3)
   b) A good start --- but you're in the Compassion Trap here (1)
   c) Are you really neglectful? The Compassion Trap again. (0)
   d) You avoided the Compassion Trap, but stepped into the Aggression Trap! (0)

Add up your total points and gauge the extent of *your* Compassion Trap:

14+: We couldn't ask for more. You can choose what to do without being trapped. Be on the lookout, though, for other situations that may trap you.

9-13: You can avoid the Compassion Trap most of the time, and you're moving in the right direction. Give some extra attention to the people and situations that continue to trap you, and attempt more assertive ways of handling them.

2-8: Consider the price you pay when you do things at the expense of your own happiness. With some practice, you *can* leave the Compassion Trap and *enjoy* what you *choose* to do. Be an assertive woman and be loved for it.

WHEN THE GOING GETS TOUGH... A NOTE ON DOMESTIC VIOLENCE

The numbers ---- and the damage ---- are staggering. It's almost like cancer.

A million women seek medical treatment for domestic violence each year. Think for a moment about how many victims *do not* seek treatment...

Battering is the single major cause of injury to women, even more significant than the number injured in car accidents, rapes and muggings combined. And it gets worse. Nearly half of all female murder victims in this country are killed by a husband or boyfriend. If that's not enough to get your attention, consider that in over one-third of families where spousal abuse occurs, child abuse is also present.

We're talking about serious physical injury or death, but even those numbers don't tell the whole story. Domestic violence can be sexual and psychological. Sexual violence takes the form of spousal rape (illegal in nearly all states) or other sexual activity forced on an unwilling victim. Psychological violence ---- efforts to make a person powerless by controlling her thinking and/or behavior ---- is more subtle, but it can be just as devastating to the victim.

What Can You Do?

The two most important things you can do about domestic violence are to *recognize it early* and *put a stop to it immediately*. Easier said than done, of course, but you can improve your chances to survive if you'll follow the steps outlined below:

1. **Start by assuming that *if you think you're being abused, you probably are.***

2. **Make an honest assessment of your circumstances, considering physical, psychological, sexual violence. Warning signs to watch for:**
   * Have you been struck physically?
   * Has it happened more than twice?
   * Is your partner extremely jealous, perhaps attempting to control your life, your activities, your contact with friends and family?
   * Have you ---- or those you care about ---- been threatened if you tell anyone?
   * Have you been forced into any sexual activity you didn't want?

* Are others in danger (e.g., children, family)?
* Does your partner use alcohol or other drugs to excess, and/or get drunk/high often?
* How violent is your partner?
* Is he rational?
* Has he hurt others in the past?

3. Consider your options:
* You can try to continue putting up with it. (Not recommended)
* You can try to fight back. (Not recommended)
* You can report him to the police. (A good idea)
* You can walk out. (Another good idea)

4. Identify your resources:
* Your own strength.
* Family members who are available to help.
* Friends who are available to help.
* A local Women's Shelter or other safe house.
* Law enforcement agencies.

5. Act Now. Don't assume "things will get better."

6. What would assertive action be?
* At the earliest sign: Confront and set limits.
* In case of violent attack: Seek professional intervention. Get out if necessary.
* In case of repeat attack: Get out now.

7. Consider carefully the consequences of any action plan:
* Have you thought carefully about the pros and cons of your plan?
* Have you consulted an attorney, law enforcement official, or protective services agency regarding your options and rights?
* Have you figured out where you can be safe?
* Can you leave secretly, without being found?
* Will you inform anyone of your plan?
* Will anyone else be in danger (e.g., your children)?
* Are you willing to press charges and face him in court?

Suggested Reading

Defending Our Lives: Getting Away from Domestic Violence and Staying Safe by Susan Murphy-Milano. New York: Anchor Books /Double-day, 1996.

Learning to Live Without Violence: A Handbook for Men by Daniel J. Sonkin, Ph.D. and Michael Durphy, M.D. Volcano, California: Volcano Press, 1989.

The Battered Woman by Lenore E. Walker, Ph.D. New York: Harper-Collins, 1979.

Notes:

Many authorities recommend getting out of a physically abusive situation at the very first incidence. Certainly if your health and safety is endangered, this is a wise choice. Obviously, each circumstance is unique. Seek professional guidance in order to make the best decisions for your life. It is possible that counseling may improve the situation, however, staying in an abusive relationship could be dangerous — even fatal... *Seek help.*

In this discussion, we have identified the perpetrator as "he," since there is considerable evidence that the vast majority of serious domestic violence victims are women who have been attacked by their male partners.

Chapter 8

Empowering Yourself To Be Assertive

I feel that I am an assertive woman in many ways now. But the problems that I am dealing with occur from a lack of confidence within myself.

— Marketing Administrator, married, in her thirties.

Ever since Eve's temptation of Adam resulted in banishment from the Garden of Eden, women have learned to be accessible to blame.

Apology and powerlessness have characterized the lives of women for generations. A woman's traditional role has been dependent, submissive: women have been expected to react rather than act, to have decisions made for them rather than make decisions for themselves. What women deserve is the power to determine the course of their own lives without apology, to make their own decisions, and to be free from the absolute authority of others.

Stereotypes start early. We hear jokes about mothers-in-law being to blame for family conflict; Jewish mothers being responsible for fostering helplessness and dependency in their children; women school teachers making "sissies" of little boys. Women have been so involved in defending themselves against these accusations that they have rarely questioned their legitimacy. Instead, they have reacted with guilt and apology, and they have transported these feelings to many other situations. Sound familiar?

Developing Your Sense of Power

This chapter is concerned with helping you to develop your sense of personal power. Personal power is so important to effective assertive behavior that it deserves our special emphasis and your alert attention.

The issue of power is beginning to assume new importance. There are two major aspects of personal power for women: how to get it and keep it, and attitudes about having it and using it.

Personal power is something we all need. Yet women have been denied the opportunity to exercise power; they have been told it isn't natural or feminine for them to want it. They have swallowed their anxiety, buried their anger, and experienced the personal anguish and disappointment produced by powerlessness and non-assertion.

We neither insist upon nor object to women competing with men for success, money, prestige, or authority ---- the external barometers of power. Instead, we are concerned with power as a positive, creative force that helps you choose for yourself, gives you a feeling of worth and purpose, and fosters a strong conviction to overcome feelings of anxiety and helplessness.

The Tools of Power

Your mind is one of the most powerful forces on earth. It can be your strongest ally or your worst enemy. How often have you imagined failure and fulfilled that negative expectation? What would happen if you put as much creativity and emotional energy into picturing *success?* Here is a set of tools to enhance the part your mind plays in becoming assertive.

Imaging. This process couples visualization ---- creating images in your mind as if what you imagine is already happening ---- with the emotional desire to make it happen. If your image has been chosen from your inner wisdom while you're in a relaxed frame of mind, it can become real in your life quickly and solidly. Regular practice of positive imagery will enable you to reproduce the pictures in your mind as real-life results.

To *become* an assertive woman, create a vivid picture in your mind of how you would *look, think,* and *feel* as an assertive woman. Create the assertive you that you want. Concentrate on this image in moments of relaxation. Fix it in your mind.

If you are uncertain that you can create your own images, ask a friend to do a guided imagery exercise with you. As you relax, perhaps with your eyes closed, have your friend vividly describe to you an image ---- in specific detail ---- that you want to have of yourself. This can be done in story-like fashion or can be related to a real situation in your life. Give your friend as much information as you can about your desired result. The more detailed your goal, the better and faster it can be achieved.

Meditation and Relaxation. There are many forms of meditation and relaxation, from a simple walk on the beach or bubble bath to the discipline Transcendental or Zen meditation, Tai Chi Ch'uan (a moving meditation, a way of learning to center and balance one's energies), and deep muscle relaxation (as discussed in Chapter 11). These approaches work to free the body and mind from stress while expanding the capacity to freely contemplate, feel joy, create. In each case, you remain awake and peaceful. The point is not to relax to the point of indifference, but to become fully open and alert to new possibilities.

Once in a meditative or relaxed state, you can give your attention to whatever you choose. You could, for example, empower yourself to work on a particular goal in becoming more assertive. If you don't know what you want as you are going into meditation or relaxation, be patient and ask your inner wisdom to guide you. Trust that you are the source of direction for your life as you want it to be, that you are in control and not being controlled. Just realizing that you have the power to be assertive will move you closer to positive action.

Affirming. In Chapter 6, we introduced Ms. Protecto, that defensive inner voice that constantly feeds us messages to direct our behavior. Affirming can keep Ms. Protecto from ruling your inner self and causing you to act non-assertively or aggressively.

Affirming is a way to be assertive with yourself. It is a creative, conscious process that enables you to express yourself more fully and confidently. An *affirmation* is a spoken and written declaration of something you want, phrased as if it were already happening. By your statement you are planting a powerful, positive suggestion in your mind. Repeating it many times daily reinforces it. The more intensely you imagine it and create an emotional experience of it (rather than repeating it blandly) the better it works.

It is important to phrase your affirmations in a positive, proactive way. For example, "I am becoming more assertive with my boss" is better than "My boss doesn't bug me." Don't pressure yourself for instant results. State your affirmations as concrete, achievable steps toward your goal. If things change gradually, the change is often more lasting and appropriate.

Allow things to happen naturally and allow yourself to be surprised, especially when something turns out better than your wildest dreams!

Another way to express your affirmations aloud is to tape record them and listen to them while driving, at home, or during coffee breaks at work. You can also include affirmations during meditations. You can tape them on your mirror or put them anywhere you look frequently. If there is a particular song or piece of music that makes you feel strong, it is helpful to record it along with your affirmations, or even sing your affirmations to its tune.

AFFIRMATIONS FOR AN ASSERTIVE WOMAN
* I am becoming an assertive woman from the inside out.
* I am dissolving the barriers to my self-expression.
* I feel more powerful.
* I communicate more clearly and effectively.
* I handle confrontations with greater ease.
* I express my enthusiasm and joy more freely and fully.
* I am becoming stronger and more courageous.
* I am more and more pleased with who I am.
* I am taking charge of my life.
* I can create love, success and happiness for myself.

Music. A powerful way to communicate with our inner selves, music reaches us at such a deep level that at times it almost seems possible to feel it rearranging our molecules! It is definitely felt in the body as it is perceived in the mind. Because it has the capacity to move the emotions so strongly, it is also a tool of empowerment. Movies use strong musical sound tracks to amplify the action. In some instances the music precedes the action; we can sense what's coming before it happens.

Other examples of how music magnifies our experiences include church services, weddings, concerts, or majestic ceremonies. We take music for granted as an integral part of our outward lives. Why not use its power in our inner lives?

Explore your own music collection for inspiration. Observe how others use music. Experiment. If you're depressed, instead of playing Gregorian chants or moody lost-love songs, try your assertiveness selection and see what happens.

Treasure Maps. Perhaps the most playful tool is the treasure map. A visual tool that makes it easier for you to picture what you want, a treasure map is a more concrete way of telling your inner self what it needs to do to achieve your goals.

A colorful drawing or collage that represents what you want can include all the things necessary to achieve your goal ---- much like scale drawings and models help architects and builders get the job done.

To create an effective treasure map, use colorful pictures, photos or drawings to display what you want in detail. These can be glued or taped to poster board or any size or type of paper you prefer, small enough to carry with you or large enough to cover an entire wall. You might place a recent photo of yourself in the map as a symbol of your ability and power to achieve your goal. Keep the design simple and real enough to maintain clarity. Include anyone or anything else that you feel is necessary: money (play money will do); another person's photo; a symbol of a higher source (to acknowledge your faith in God or the universe). Spend a few moments every day quietly contemplating your treasure map, preferably at the beginning and the end of your day.

Power Grabbers

The assertive woman knows that the best way to protect her rights is to use them. Yet, many women have trouble developing confidence in their own power. Becoming comfortable with power and enjoying a feeling of competence will take some practice. By practicing with the exercises and examples in this chapter, you can develop an assertive attitude and experience a feeling of being in control.

Before attempting each situation, relax and imagine yourself successfully completing the exercise. After you are able to do that without feeling anxious, try it out alone in front of a mirror. Then you are ready to try it with a friend with whom you feel comfortable, or in a relatively low risk situation. Do not push yourself too fast, and don't try to be assertive with an intimidating person, or in an uncomfortable situation, until you have mastered relaxation and successful imaging.

The Need for Approval. Working for others' approval limits your autonomy because you voluntarily concede your power to someone else. Dorrie Doormat, for example, is a reliable, responsible employee. She makes decisions, but once she's made them, she presents them to someone else because she wants that person to tell her she's done a good job, to give her approval. Allison Assertive can make decisions without the need to present them to someone else. She uses her own power and resists seeking the familiar comfort of approval. Her autonomy and personal power are more important to her. As an assertive woman, Allison stands up for what she believes, and makes decisions independently for herself.

"I'm Sorry, But..." Many women find themselves struggling against years of apology. The phrase "I'm sorry, but..." is a common refrain. Women frequently feel compelled to apologize for saying "no," for exercising their authority, for expressing their anger or when asking for something. A woman's inappropriate use of apology reflects her feelings of powerlessness, indecisiveness, and ambivalence about whether or not she even has the right to make a request, or to disagree. When women apologize unnecessarily, they are really saying, "I know I don't have the right to say this, and I don't want to bother you with it, and I'm sorry for saying it, but..."

There are, of course, legitimate and appropriate times for an apology. The legitimate apology conveys understanding and appreciation of another person's feelings, such as "I'm very sorry I was late; I must have kept you waiting for an hour." The examples below illustrate inappropriate and appropriate uses of apology.

"GUESS WHO'S COMING TO DINNER?"

Scenario: Dorrie Doormat has invited several women to her home for dinner this evening at 7 p.m. They finally arrive at 9, two hours late. The dinner Dorrie prepared is cold and ruined. One of her guests, Augusta, is critical.

Augusta: "Weren't we invited for dinner, Dorrie? You didn't plan very well, did you?"

Dorrie: "Oh, I'm so sorry, Augusta! I feel just awful about this. I'm really sorry to cause such an inconvenience."

In this situation, Dorrie apologizes inappropriately. It is Augusta and the other guests who caused Dorrie the inconvenience by arriving late. The apology should have come from them.

"DINNER IS SERVED — LATE"

Scenario: Allison Assertive has invited two of her friends to dinner at 7 p.m. She is late coming home, and doesn't arrive until 6:45. When her friends arrive at 7, Allison is just preparing dinner, which won't be ready until 8.

Allison: "I'm really sorry that dinner will be late. You must be absolutely starving. How about some cheese and crackers, while we're waiting?"

In this case, Allison apologizes legitimately to her friends for the late dinner. She acknowledges that they must be hungry and makes a positive suggestion, but she does not over-apologize.

The next time you find yourself apologizing, ask yourself what you are apologizing for:
* Was the apology legitimate and appropriate?
* Did you feel compelled to apologize?
* Did you apologize for something even though you had nothing to be sorry about?

Getting Your Questions Answered

Have you ever asked an important question, only to be sidetracked when someone else changes the subject to avoid answering you? If so, you probably felt frustrated and confused.

Try the following outline to help you to exercise some control and get your questions answered:

1. Start with a brief, specific question.

2. Picture yourself asking this question of a person you feel comfortable with, and as you do, practice relaxation.

3. Put step (2) into action, and ask a friend your question. Instruct your friend to try to avoid answering by every means possible until she feels she has run out of excuses and evasions. Each time she gives another rationalization, continue to ask the question as if it were the first time it was asked, without varying your voice tone.

4. If you don't receive an appropriate answer, precede your question with "I will repeat the question," or a similar neutral statement, followed by the question.

5. If your friend responds with a *feeling* instead of an answer to your question, *acknowledge* the feeling, but continue to repeat your question.

6. When a direct answer is given, acknowledge the answer in a neutral, non-judgmental way, "Thank you for telling me."

7. If your friend makes insulting or other negative remarks, you may follow your acknowledgement by telling her how you feel about these remarks. You can do this assertively, without punishing your friend for not answering you honestly. What you are concerned with is your right to exercise your power to have your questions answered. So, remember

the assertive woman remains non-judgmental and non-abusive, and keeps her voice evenly modulated — not loud or angry.

"ARE YOU HAVING AN AFFAIR?"

A situation that frequently comes up in seminars involves confronting a lover whom one suspects of having an affair. The woman has usually experienced a great deal of emotional pain, and has attempted to deal with it by ignoring it, playing the martyr, or by fighting fire with fire. At this point, she is ready to try the alternative of being assertive. The following dialogue illustrates a classic assertive response to this emotionally-charged situation. Each woman must tailor her response to her own needs and style; this may mean that her assertiveness is interrupted by angry outbursts or tears. Remember that to be assertive does not mean to be perfect.

Allison: "I have been concerned lately about the amount of time you are away from home. You have been telling me that you are busy and have to work late, but I have the feeling you are holding back on me. Are you having an affair?"

Lover: "Don't be ridiculous. I've got important work to do. It takes too much time to explain it to you. You don't understand."

Allison: "I feel you're being evasive with me, and I'm very concerned about what's happening. I will repeat my question. Are you having an affair?"

Lover: "How many times have I told you not to bug me with your stupid questions? I'm really angry! Why don't you trust me?"

Allison: "I know that you're angry about my asking you the same question over again. I really do want to trust you, and I can when you are open with me. I'd feel more comfortable knowing the truth and being given the choice to deal with it, rather than being in the dark and feeling anxious and insecure. I would like to know if you are having an affair."

Lover: "You really know how to back somebody up against the wall, don't you? You must really get a kick out of playing Sherlock Holmes. I've had enough of your nagging. How do you think it makes me feel to be interrogated like this and subjected to your high pressure tactics? I suppose your friends put you up to this."

Allison: "I want you to feel comfortable about discussing this with me. The last thing I want to do is threaten you. It is really important to me to clear up this distance between us. I would like to know where I stand, so it is very important for me to know if you're having an affair. Are you?"

Lover: "Well, just remember that you asked for it! Yes, I am having an affair. I hope you're happy now that you squeezed it out of me."

Allison: "I appreciate your telling me, even though it doesn't make me happy to know that you're having an affair. I feel at least now we can begin an honest discussion of our relationship."

Remember that the content in this exercise is extremely meaningful. It is important to choose words that are not accusatory, for example by saying, "I feel" instead of "you make me feel." Even though the other person may insult you, it is important to be concerned with your feelings rather than letting yourself get sidetracked by name-calling or other manipulative devices.

You have a right to ask questions and to expect direct answers, and you should give such answers yourself. However, there are times when you will not want to be forced to answer questions. Assertiveness gives you the power to decide.

Choosing Not to Answer Questions

Now that you have practiced getting your questions answered, consider what to do when you are in the opposite position. How do you respond when someone is asking *you* a question you don't want to answer? Perhaps the question is irrelevant, embarrassing, or intimidating. How do you handle this situation? Try a method that has worked for us.

First, be sure you understand the question. If you do not, then clarify it by repeating it back to your questioner. Once it is clear and you still do not feel comfortable answering, make a simple, direct statement saying that you do not want to answer it. If your interrogator persists, you might express how you feel about the question or the persistence of the questioner. Then repeat again that you do not want to answer the question.

"WHERE HAVE YOU BEEN . . .?"

Scenario: A single woman just took a few days off from work to have an abortion. There are a couple of curious co-workers who seem intent on discovering the reason for her absence.

Nosey: "Oh, Allison, you look a little pale. You must have been pretty sick to have stayed out for three days. Would you like to talk about it?"

Allison: "I'm not sure what you mean by 'it.' Could you be a little more specific?"

Nosey: "Well, some of us noticed that you were nauseated a few mornings here at work. And your clothes didn't seem to be fitting quite the same, if you know what I mean. Well, what I'm trying to say is — Allison, did you have an abortion?"

Allison: "I really feel uncomfortable with your asking me what I feel is a very personal question, and I don't want to answer it."

Nosey: "Of course, I know it is rather personal, but we're asking only because we care about you. Is there anything we can do?"

Allison: "It really makes me angry for you to persist in prying into my personal life. I do not feel it is necessary to answer your question."

Nosey: "I don't see why not. Everybody knows anyway."

Allison: "I don't want to discuss your question any further. I am going to resume working, which is what we ought to be doing, anyway."

Write down three questions that you anticipate being asked that you do not want to answer. Then role-play the situation and practice *not* answering the question by using the process described here.

"SURE, NO PROBLEM"

Scenario: We had hoped and expected that some of the stereotypic boss-secretary problems would no longer exist in the late 1990s. Unfortunately, the topic still comes up quite frequently in our women's classes, especially with secretaries and administrative assistants.

The boss (usually male) has just asked his secretary if she wouldn't mind during her lunch break exchanging some merchandise his wife bought. He then adds that he'd like her to try to get back from lunch *early* because he has some extra word processing for her that must be done right away. She wants to tell him that she is not going to do it.

Dorrie: "Oh, *I'm sorry, but* I was going to have lunch with a friend I haven't seen in years who's in town for the day. But, I guess I could call her and cancel our plans. Yes, I guess I'll do that. Sure, it's no problem. Where do you want me to go?"

Allison: "I've made plans with a good friend that I haven't seen in years. She will only be in town today, and it is very important that I see her. I know that you are rushed. I can work on the document as soon as I return; we'll get it out in time. Returning the gift is different. I am uncomfortable running your personal errands and I must refuse. You can count on me to pitch in with office business, of course."

"DO YOU HAVE THE NERVE?"

Here is another action exercise we have developed to help you to gain confidence in taking the initiative ---- by acting instead of waiting to react. Choose at least three out of the five following situations and rank them according to how uncomfortable the thought of doing them makes you feel, A being the *least* uncomfortable and F being the *most* uncomfortable. Then, starting with A, decide how you are going to go about doing something active about it instead of waiting to see what the other person does. You can write a script before you try it or role-play what you are going to say first. Try to visualize what your "ideal" assertive woman would do:

• Make an appointment with your employer, teacher, or family to let them know that you feel you are doing a fine job, instead of waiting for someone to notice.

• Your children are bugging you. You take responsibility for telling them how you are feeling and that you want them to stop bothering you right now. Do *not* threaten them with "Wait until your father hears about this," do not wait until somebody else takes the responsibility, do not react with pent-up frustration and complaints.

• Call a woman or a man whom you have never called about something you want to tell her/him instead of waiting for her/him to call you.

• Somebody makes a request of you, perhaps to borrow something or to ask a favor. If you do not feel like loaning it or doing it, say so right away instead of letting your anxiety build.

• You want to talk to your lover/mate about an important feeling you have, perhaps about sex. Set up the right time and place and initiate the conversation. Do not passively wait for the right time and place to happen, or for your partner to talk about it first.

• Return a defective item to the store, even though you don't have the sales slip, or you have procrastinated for weeks about returning it.

Power is as much a feeling of confidence from within as it is an outward display of your effectiveness in getting what you want. In fact, you can feel powerful even when you don't get what you want.

Empowering yourself to be assertive is a long term investment that pays off. When you commit to being assertive from the inside out, you win. You can learn from your losses, let go gracefully, and move with confidence to whatever challenge awaits you.

Suggested Reading

The Artist's Way: A Spiritual Path to Higher Creativity, by Julia Cameron with Mark Bryan. New York: Jeremy Tarcher/Putnam Book, 1992.

Wishcraft: How to Get What You Really Want, by Barbara Sher. New York: Ballantine Books, 1986.

Chapter 9

The Expression of Assertion

I had a real test of my own assertiveness. I had gotten a quote from the printer on the cost of new brochures. When it came time to order, however, the price was double the original quotation.

I believe the first thing I did was break out in a sweat! After I had given him my side of it, he insisted that the second price had to stand. I suddenly had a flash which said ---- silence will solve this.

So I sat tight, he squirmed, I got the original price.

What more can be said about how assertiveness is expressed? Over the past two decades ---- and from all indications well into the next ---- thousands of articles, quizzes, books, how-to guides, seminars, workshops, classes, and lectures have been designed to help people become more assertive, less aggressive; more confident, less afraid; more effective, less wishy-washy. To be able to express oneself assertively ---- to stand up to bullies, defend one's position, congratulate a colleague on a job well done, ask a new person out ---- became the goal of the non-assertive over the years. To speak up when it mattered most ---- that was the idea.

Along the way, we discovered there's a difference between using assertiveness as a *method* to accomplish a goal, and the longer term prospect of developing an assertive *identity*. As a method, assertiveness is available to anyone ---- you don't have to think of yourself as assertive to be able to use it successfully. Someone who has trouble expressing a conflicting point of view among friends, say, may nonetheless be quite good at dispatching the vacuum cleaner salesperson at the door. The assertive identity part —— assertiveness is your middle name, finding that assertive responses outnumber the rest —— well, that's something else again.

Assertiveness was, in the beginning, a way of confronting the unpleasant or difficult without getting squashed (or squashing others) in the process. Newly honed assertive skills were plied on waiters ("I ordered this steak well-done. It's quite rare. Please take it back and bring me a well-done steak"), on spouses ("When you interrupt me, I get frustrated and angry"), on cold-calling salespeople ("No, I do not want to buy a set of porcelain corncob skewers"), and on bosses ("I am willing to work overtime as long as I am paid to do so"). The keynote, usually, was standing one's ground, and firmly. An early objective was to find out how good we were at asking —— and then standing up —— for what we wanted. We practiced saying and doing the things that gave us sweaty palms and cold feet until we could perform them with a certain amount of comfort. It got easier as we went along.

After a while, we realized that using assertiveness the way you might use any handy tool left something to be desired. In some university extension classrooms, "Assertive Skills Workshops" produced cookie-cutter responses to the top ten situations in which assertiveness was the antidote. The techniques learned there were neither universally accepted nor admired, as we quickly saw when we tried them out in the real world. At the same time, even partly successful assertive encounters produced a rush of pride. It could be done! We lived to tell about it! Honoring our own wishes didn't mean turning our backs on friends!

One Size Does Not Fit All

It was especially gratifying to learn that there was no such thing as an "ideal" or "perfect" way to be assertive —— no pressure to live up to that perfect assertive woman image —— but instead there were many legitimate variations of assertive expression. Those who considered themselves shy by nature were relieved to discover they could express themselves assertively without feeling phony, acting a part. Their style was simply a little softer, a little toned down —— but without hesitation, insecurity, and without apology. The more extroverted discovered that they, too, could weave assertiveness into their own unique expansiveness with good results. They didn't have to give up any of their exuberance for the sake of assertive communication. Women who had always thought of themselves as spontaneous and daring were delighted to see that assertiveness didn't require putting a damper on their intensity, or make them less interesting. Assertiveness could actually enhance the things we liked best about ourselves. We could get what we wanted and we could be nice about it. Little by little, we imagined assertiveness not as a checklist of behaviors which we had to perform competently, but as a natural extension of our own personalities, with all our differences, preferences, and eccentricities.

Think of Madeleine Albright, who, after serving four years as U.S. Ambassador to the United Nations, was named Secretary of State in 1997 ---- the first woman ever to get the job. Tenacious and tough-minded, Albright lost no time in showing that she was very much her own woman. On the day her appointment was announced, she let everybody know she was not her predecessor, Warren Christopher: "I hope my heels can fill his shoes," she joked. Meanwhile, at Mattel, president and CEO Jill Barad (the first woman CEO of a Fortune 500 company who got there entirely on her own) makes sure that almost a hundred new Barbies ---- among them an astronaut, a vet, even a military commando ---- are introduced each year. Thanks to Barad's innovations, in 1995, Barbie brought in $1.4 billion in sales, which is only one of the reasons Barad now sits on the board of Microsoft. And in 1996, Linda Chavez-Thompson became the first woman executive vice-president of the 13-million member, 110-year old AFL-CIO. The Texas-born Chavez-Thompson, who describes herself as a "pushy broad," won the labor coalition's top spot after working her way up through the ranks as a labor organizer.

Each of these women has, in her own way, changed the world. It's silly to debate whether certain high-profile figures are interchangeable (of course they're not), or even whether they are really, truly assertive models (that's in the eye of the beholder, as always). Assertiveness can ---- and should ---- be expressed differently from one person to the next, and that's something to encourage. Nobody, for example, should assume that Chavez-Thompson could take over for Barad, just because both women happen to be gifted, direct and assertive. It is that certain mix of personality, talent, interests, and moxie that defines who your own assertive woman will be.

Let's not confuse assertiveness, a skill that thrives on individual differences, with, say, championship figure-skating or Greco-Roman wrestling, where nothing counts so much as flawless form. Out here in the real world, it hardly matters that you are not perfectly assertive; you might prefer, on some days, to stay in your pajamas and forget about living up to your "assertiveness potential" altogether. Get to the point where you can say, from your gut, that you are not an assertive android who has been programmed to look out for You-Know-Who, no matter what. You don't need charisma or a magnetic personality. Assertiveness can settle in and become a part of you, just the way you are. It can make the good better and impart a sheen to the lackluster. It makes you courageous.

The more we thought about it, we saw that the process of assertiveness gets better with time: the newly-assertive woman may stumble, unsure of herself because she's still testing and discovering how this works. After a while, the assertive woman begins to learn that she's the one in charge. It's up to her to say when and where and how to assert herself, but she doesn't have to merely because she knows how.

Side Trips

We've learned that moving from the early learning stages to being able to claim assertiveness as one of one's personal characteristics is a process with certain predictable features. As you build confidence in your own ability to be assertive, you become acquainted with some specific side trips or traps on the way. Part of the process is to recognize them and move on.

We think psychotherapist Andrew Salter was the first to point out that what often passed as assertive expression actually was not. As much as twenty years before assertiveness gained acceptance in circles outside therapy groups, Salter described variations of what he called "fraudulent assertion," including "fake assertion," "actor's assertion," and "manipulative assertion." Salter correctly observed that fraudulent assertion involves "...no search for accommodation. It's just a disguised steamroller." He characterized actor's assertion as a sort of stream of hail-fellow-well-met greetings ---- "Hello, how are you, good to see you," all delivered in a "slightly breathless" manner. Manipulative assertion is "dishonest, not real assertion in the first place." Last, he included a brief mention of "Pollyanna assertion," where everything is "just great, just dandy." We have adapted Salter's descriptions to take a closer look at four popular side-trips on the way to becoming an assertive woman: Reckless Assertion, Pollyanna Assertion, Fraudulent Assertion, and the Superwoman Syndrome.

Reckless Assertion

You made it through a prickly encounter with a hostile person. You initiated a difficult conversation. You pushed for a point of view you believed in. You didn't cave in when criticized by someone whose opinions you care about. That first flush of victory is heady stuff. You want to do it again. Another chance to assert yourself is just around the corner, each success more encouraging than the last. As long as you and others agree that you are doing something worthwhile, a little overkill is okay by your pals; the recklessly assertive carry it too far.

As they watch your self-assurance give way to recklessness, even the most tolerant of your friends will have misgivings about your tactics. To be "recklessly assertive," as we call it, is to rashly plunge ahead ever more assertively, with little or no attention paid to the consequences or dangers involved.

Most authorities would argue that if you are not in tune with the consequences of your assertive actions, you really aren't being assertive. In practice, however, we find that the process of learning to be assertive usually involves at least one detour into recklessness. It's not that you are so fired up with newfound power that you want to steamroll everyone you see. It's that you are still new at this assertiveness business, and your judgment about what is appropriately assertive behavior isn't as good as it will be: for now, you may not notice or take seriously the fact that your constant assertiveness wears thin with some.

That's the problem faced by many working women who want to project a professional image, especially if they have just been hired. They feel real pressure to perform better than expected and to make few mistakes, which they suspect would not be easily forgiven or forgotten. If they express too many traditional feminine behaviors, they jeopardize their hard-won status by "acting like wimps." They believe they must never let anyone catch them behaving as anything less than strong, assertive professionals.

So how can recklessness be overcome and self-assurance rediscovered? The first step is to slow down enough to see that the independence and capability that has served you well so far need not be relentlessly proved. The advice and counsel of someone more experienced might help you understand how you can be more effective. Such a person can provide a more realistic, practical perspective, especially if she has been through it herself. You'll also learn an important lesson in assertiveness: you have to be sensitive to, but not enslaved by, others' perceptions of your behavior. You are free to reject their assessment, of course. But consider that they may know something that you don't.

The dangers of reckless assertion can be diluted if you can be receptive to feedback from others. You can tackle some of the job yourself by taking the time to reflect on the situations that bring out your fighting instinct. What circumstances seem to fuel reckless assertion? How might the situation have been resolved if you had behaved differently? When do you feel most defensive? Has reckless assertion damaged your credibility? Your answers can help to short-circuit what might become a persistent pattern.

Reckless Assertion: Does She or Doesn't She?

Here's a list of significant behaviors and ways of getting things done that might indicate recklessness. The more you believe the statements apply to your approach, the more likely it is that you've detoured into reckless assertion.

* It seems that you nearly always take the lead in your relationships with others.
* Friends are telling you that you're defensive or argumentative.
* It's more important that you get what *you* want in the end than it is to go along with what others want.
* To describe you as a "fist in a velvet glove" would be about right.
* You crave being the center of attention.
* After so many years as a pushover, it is exhilarating to finally be able to turn the tables.
* Though you can be direct and assertive with different people, they don't seem to want to see as much of you as before.
* There are certain specific instances which ignite your anger to the point you cannot control your outbursts.
* Compared to other people you know, you are much more likely to persevere to get what you want.
* People tell you that you never give up, or that you are incredibly singleminded.
* You find it extremely difficult to apologize even when an apology is called for.
* Winning isn't everything: it's the only thing.
* You resent others' good fortune.
* You find that you cannot predict how other people will react to your assertiveness.

* You feel that you do not get the recognition you deserve in life.
* You aren't comfortable playing a purely supportive role at times with your spouse or friends.
* You believe that if you don't look out for your own interests, nobody else will.
* People tell you that you have a forceful personality.
* You are not as flexible as some other people you know.
* You cannot tell when your assertiveness wears thin with some people.
* In general, people tend to let you down.

Pollyanna Assertion

Like the storybook character, everything is just peachy with Pollyanna ---- on the outside, at least. On the inside we have a different story indeed.

Pollyanna assertion comes from the mouths of those who think of themselves as passive, non-assertive people. It's the Pollyanna in you who is overfocused on "acceptable assertions," the ones that may be enthusiastically received because they pose no challenge or threat to anyone else. Pollyanna assertion has to do with wanting to be accepted, with wanting to fit in. The main focus of your attention is still what's going on around you, with less, if any, allegiance to how you feel about it and how you might change or contribute to it. Like the Compassion Trap, Pollyanna assertion attaches more importance to making room for others' opinions and preferences than it does to honoring your own.

We don't suggest that this class of assertive responses ---- expressing agreement, support, love, appreciation, praise, or enthusiasm ---- has less value than some of the others, including giving critical feedback, expressing a discordant point of view, or expressing anger. Both sets are available to the assertive woman, but Pollyanna is uncomfortable with all but the "nice" ones. She likes to be assertive, but safely so, mostly within limits (usually determined by others). She may be willing to take the first step, but only when she knows she's expressing the majority view. At the first sign of disagreement, she is likely to back down and revert to passive behaviors.

A friend discovered that Pollyannaism damaged her effectiveness in her first supervisory job. She was promoted for her proven ability to get along with her peers. She could always be counted on to pitch in and to set a new, more productive standard for her group. When she hit management, however, she encountered problems. She would go into salary reviews armed with responsible proposals for increases for her people, but her recommendations were seldom reflected in the increases that were approved by top management. She watched as other supervisors received approvals for their recommended increases, and she couldn't understand why her proposals had been "singled out," as she put it. Worse, her people began to question her ability to represent their interests to higher-ups.

It took some time and soul-searching, but she began to see that while she genuinely wanted to take care of her team, she had trouble standing up for them when she felt the most pressure to perform: in front of senior executives. She had no difficulty providing assertive support for her team or in handling touchy situations, like arranging vacation schedules when several key people wanted the same weeks off. But when she faced those executives, she was too quick to accept their counterproposals. She didn't realize that as a supervisor, she was expected to defend her recommendations. Instead, she interpreted the executive's responses as the last word on the subject. She judged it best to cut her losses and try to find some way to explain the disappointing result to her team, which was, to put it mildly, profoundly unsatisfactory.

Our friend behaved assertively, to a point. She could be assertive in situations where she didn't have to ask for too much, but would seek familiar, passive ground when the going got tough. Although she did not agree with the executives' decision, she tried her best to put a smile on her face and accept it as she thought a "real team player" should. She would simply have to hunker down and try harder next time to come up with a better, more carefully thought-out proposal. In the meantime, her Pollyanna assertion was earning her an unwanted reputation for being politically naive and ineffective in management.

Pollyanna assertion is incomplete. It goes only as far as custom will allow. It can be a legitimate option, but it never works as a consistent strategy. What could our friend have done to get out of the Pollyanna trap? She could have listened to what the executives had to say, and calmly reiterated the reasons why her recommendations should stand. It goes without saying that she was fully prepared for this meeting, and could have produced reams of data to support her position. Armed with the information she needed and the willingness to confront her fears of rejection directly, she would likely have won the raises she asked for.

Which is exactly what she did the next time around.

Pollyanna Assertion: Does She or Doesn't She?

How about you? If, in the descriptions that follow, you see yourself ---- you also see Pollyanna. Review the chapters which seem to present the toughest challenges to your assertiveness: "Saying No," "Compliments, Criticism, and Rejection." Gradually work toward a real balance of expression, when you can be comfortable giving bad news as well as good.

* Your assertiveness has been enthusiastically received by your friends and family.
* You don't express anger directly when you feel it.
* You don't think your "negative" feelings are justified or important enough to share.
* You crave acceptance and approval.
* Authority figures continue to intimidate you.
* You are afraid of disturbing the status quo; your motto could be "leave well enough alone."
* When you and friends decide to go to a movie, you are much more likely to go along with what your friends want to see than you are to suggest a particular show.
* Stating your opinion makes you feel trapped and uncomfortable.
* It is second nature to you to be warm and encouraging of others.
* You are afraid of expressing powerful emotions.
* You consider yourself shy.
* Admitting that you are angry seems like a major imposition.
* Even when you feel depressed or anxious, you would never dream of admitting it to anyone.
* Having good manners is very important to you; you know all about etiquette.
* You are super-conscious of "overstepping your bounds."
* You want others to appreciate you.

Fraudulent Assertion

Like Pollyanna assertion, the fraudulent variety also masks an underlying fear or anxiety, but with very different tactics and results. As the name suggests, fraudulent assertion isn't assertion which takes direction from a sincerely held feeling or opinion ---- it's a fake. Often it's nothing more than thinly disguised manipulation, dressed up to look like assertiveness. At other times, it can be "textbook assertion," the kind that looks and sounds authentic, but actually covers up a hidden agenda. The assertive fraud wants to be thought assertive, but she can't really claim the part.

Fraudulent assertions are well remembered and energetically resented. Like other indirect maneuvers, they have the capacity to provoke a desire for revenge. While the "fraud" herself may be honestly unaware of any discord, those on the receiving end have a very different perspective.

But fraudulent assertiveness is not something that can be attributed to mean, vindictive, or sick people. It's not the province of a particular class of rotten individuals with deceit in their hearts. It's opportunistic. It's the desire to be assertive without the corresponding faith in oneself to live up to the responsibility assertiveness entails.

We all probably know an assertive fraud. She's the one who accepts a leadership position in her child's fourth grade parent's night committee, but telephones you the night before the big event to say that she's run into a problem and could you bake three dozen cookies by 8 a.m. tomorrow? She's the boss who urges you to spearhead a controversial task force, but when you receive heated criticism for your part in it, recedes into the background and may even publicly denounce your participation. She's the friend whose brutal, insensitive criticisms are excused with a murmured "Well, I was just being direct!" Transgressions like these might be forgiven the first time, but if it's fraudulent assertion, they are part of a pattern which tries the patience and the understanding of those left to pick up the pieces.

To the fraudulently assertive woman, assertiveness is merely a thin, if useful, veneer. Unfortunately, it's not the kind of assertiveness that inspires trust. It's the fraud who commits and the friends who have the responsibility for making good on the promises. Assertiveness isn't assertiveness without the willingness to accept responsibility for one's actions.

Fraudulent Assertion: Does She or Doesn't She?

Do you know an assertive fraud? As you review the list below, notice whether a particular person or event comes to mind. Are there special people or times that spark fraudulent assertion in you?

* Maintaining a strong, independent, assertive image to others is the most important thing to you.
* You have the tendency to beg off previous commitments at the last possible moment.

* Assertiveness seems like a useful tool which would enhance your "marketability" or attractiveness.
* You use assertiveness as permission to say anything you want to anyone at any time.
* You are more tenacious than anyone you know.
* You dismiss others' criticisms by explaining that you were "just being direct and honest."
* People have told you that you are too ambitious.
* You know how to use assertiveness to get what you want, but if it fails, you attack.
* People seem to carry grudges against you.
* You have been known to throw temper tantrums or make a scene.
* At work, people make excuses to avoid being on committees with you or working in the same area as you do.
* You feel that you have been treated unfairly in the past and have resolved never to let it happen again.
* Patience is not one of your virtues.
* You feel compelled to contribute your two cents to any discussion; if you don't, you feel cheated and frustrated.

The Superwoman Syndrome

Hands down, the most alluring, hard-to-resist trap for the assertive woman is the Superwoman. She's the one who strives to do and be everything to everybody, all the time. It's easy to understand how it happens. When you find out you're good at something, you look for new ways to apply that skill and reap the rewards. Accomplishment feels good; Superwomen don't know when to quit.

Plenty of women find out about Superwomanhood the hard way. They wake up one morning and realize that there is always one more job to do, one more ball to juggle, and they come up short. An assertive woman can open all kinds of new and inspiring doors, but when she grabs for every opportunity each day presents, she soon discovers there's only one remedy: She's got to get a life.

It's a special trap that assertiveness can bring, the woman who does it all — and well, too. We cover it in more detail in the "Assertiveness Works at Work" chapter. Suffice it to say here that the desire to be a Superwoman sneaks up on you before you know it. It's the wish to be the best you can be gone awry. Assertiveness becomes your obligation, not your choice. Every opportunity carries the expectation that you will surmount any difficulties and succeed in spite of it all. That, in itself, isn't so bad. It's when the obligations overwhelm you, leaving you limp and weary, that life as a Superwoman shows its true colors.

The fulfilling part of becoming assertive is the new options and choices and sense of accomplishment that come with it. You can do things you couldn't imagine yourself doing before, and do them with style. The successes you are enjoying may make it hard to see the hazards that line the path along the way. For the Superwoman, the chief hazard is simply the variety of new and enticing choices! An assertive woman chooses her commitments carefully. She relies on her own judgment about what constitutes success for her. The answer you reach will be different from that of your friends, possibly even different from your own answer last year ---- but the important issue is that you understand not only that "enough is enough," but *you* are enough.

The Superwoman Syndrome: Does She or Doesn't She?

The following descriptions fit a woman who is doing a dozen things at once, but she may not realize it. If most of these descriptions apply to you, ask yourself whether you're attempting too much of a good thing.

* You feel overwhelmed by obligations and responsibilities.
* You sometimes wonder if you are going crazy.
* Lately you've been daydreaming about going off to a tropical island by yourself.
* When you don't accomplish something as well or as quickly as you expected, you punish yourself.
* You feel like a failure.
* You still cannot say no without a lot of guilt.
* You feel very different from other people you know.
* You're more susceptible to illnesses than your friends seem to be.
* You are eating too much and/or drinking too much.
* Or, conversely, you aren't eating.
* Nervous habits have a permanent home with you.
* It is impossible for you to relax.
* You grind your teeth in your sleep.
* As a girl or when you were younger, you suffered from eating disorders, such as anorexia or bulimia.
* At work, you feel so much stress that you think you will scream.
* You overreact and become harshly self-critical when you haven't returned a telephone call within a day.

* You're secretly proud of the fact that you haven't taken a vacation in years.

* You want to prove that you can cut it in this world.

* You believe that if you fail, every woman fails.

The Eye of the Beholder

Each snare ---- Reckless Assertion, Pollyanna Assertion, Fraudulent Assertion, and the Superwoman Syndrome ---- can be sidestepped with the support of friends, family members and colleagues who are willing to let you know when you've jumped off the deep end. It might sting a little, but you'll learn something about how your idea of assertiveness squares with the way your behavior actually comes across. With others' help ---- did I come off too strong there? Should I beef up my approach, or tone it down? ---- you'll develop your own good sense of direction, no compass required.

There are a lot of ways to give assertiveness a voice. Among them are the strategic use of silence (as illustrated in the epigraph which opened this chapter) and the less showy but equally effective small, daily victories that eventually move mountains. Such choices, and a thousand variations on this theme, are all part of the expression of assertion.

Chapter 10

You're Worth It!

Nobody can make you feel inferior without your consent.
---- Eleanor Roosevelt

T he lion's share of knowing that "you are worth it" is being willing and able to take a stand on your own behalf. Powerlessness and diminished self-confidence are products of the passive inferiority women have accepted without complaint. In this chapter, we urge you to reject the notion of being inferior.

Self-Esteem and Confidence

Many modern women ---- even those you'd call assertive ---- feel the need to boost their self-esteem and confidence. Although women are achieving more, outdistancing previous generations of women and men, they tenaciously continue to devalue themselves and their contributions. Deep down (or maybe not so deep), they still buy into a persistent cultural view of women as the inferior sex, defective physically and lacking intellectually.

It is hard work to jettison such heavy psychological cargo. Some women seek recognition and reassurance in the way they look, the number of awards they've won, the car they drive ---- everywhere but inside themselves. But self-respect never depends on winning others' approval. Every woman knows in her heart that friends and foes alike can be fooled by bravada, if her performance is carefully rehearsed. Genuine confidence, of course, is born and proven from within.

Imagine for a moment that you are at a gathering of family, friends or work associates. You have been asked to give a brief talk on "Calculating My Confidence: Knowing I'm Worth It." You accept the invitation. Here is what you say:

I KNOW I'M WORTH IT WHEN...

* I am excited about new situations.
* I believe what others say about me is their opinion —— not my worth.
* I approve of myself.
* I think and choose for myself.
* My needs and desires are important enough to make them happen.
* I share my talents and triumphs openly without embarrassment.
* I am free to express my feelings and thoughts.
* I don't measure my worth by comparisons with others.
* I accept my mistakes as useful lessons.
* I give myself credit for my efforts aimed at success, whether they succeed or not.
* I can look in the mirror with a genuine smile and say, "Hey, I really like you. You're O.K. in my book."

Did this exercise in imagination catch you off guard? How comfortable did you feel imagining yourself in this scenario? Were you able to imagine it at all? Or, did you reject it or resist it? Why? How do you feel right now about your confidence level? Are you willing to do whatever it takes to know and feel that you're worth it?

Satisfaction, Nurturance, and Bouncing Back

Knowing that you're worth it is rooted in what we call a satisfaction mentality. That's when you believe there's more to life than merely coping with problems in order to survive. Expect abundance, comfort, success, enjoyment and love. At the end of the day, let go of finished and unfinished business, relax, and look forward to another day.

One of the most challenging obstacles to self-respect is the feeling that you're downright selfish to give yourself a pat on the back (instead of waiting for a good word from somebody else). Yet nurturing yourself is just the opposite of selfishness. Selfish, self-indulgent types go for immediate, short-term highs; nurturance is the lifelong process of fostering respect for yourself and others. It is a very high form of assertiveness.

Like anything that really matters, becoming a confident, assertive woman takes time. Along the way, of course, there will be failures and disappointments. But here's a secret: the difference between the glowing success story and the crushing failure isn't luck, or fate, or intelligence; it's the ability to bounce back. For starters, it helps to remember that sometimes things look like a failure in the middle; anticipate occasional setbacks, welcome them, even, because they're ways to learn. What's important is that you get up, brush yourself off, and move forward ---- with or without a smile, but forward nonetheless.

Kara Di Giovanna understood this perfectly when she wrote the poem, "Comes the Dawn."

After a while you learn
The subtle difference
Between holding a hand
And chaining a soul.
And you learn
That love doesn't mean leaning,
And company doesn't mean security.
And you begin to learn
That kisses aren't contracts
And presents aren't promises.
And you begin to accept your defeats
With your head up and your eyes ahead
With the grace of a woman or man
Not the grief of a child.
And you learn to build all your roads on today
Because tomorrow's ground is
Too uncertain for plans
And futures have a way of falling down
In mid-flight.
After a while you learn
That even sunshine burns if you ask too much.
So you plant your own garden
And decorate your own soul
Instead of waiting for someone to bring you
Flowers.
And you learn
That you really can endure
That you really are strong
And you really do have worth.
And you learn...
And you learn...
With every failure
You learn.

A Love Letter

As an exercise in self-nurturance, sit quietly alone, perhaps play some gentle music in the background, and imagine writing to someone you love: YOU! Think about what you would say to yourself if you were someone else who could express love for you. When you feel the feelings and words flowing, begin to write a love letter to yourself. Feel free to say everything you want to say about your past, present and future. You may include observations of what you love in yourself, how great you make yourself feel, what promises you want to make to improve your life, forgiveness for past mistakes and failures, and even a loving pep talk directed toward challenges to come. Sign it with as much love and appreciation as you can feel for yourself. Keep it and read it occasionally. You can repeat this process on your birthday, at Christmas, or any time. If you feel hesitant or foolish, it's okay. Remember you are *worth* this effort and it *will* feel good.

Stand Fast

Every day, there are innumerable ways to step out and test your mettle, to stand up for what you believe is right, or to keep your cool in the face of danger. Connie Yambert, who teaches people "How to Speak with Authority" in Los Angeles, told us what it was like to come face-to-face with one of those times ---- a frightening encounter with two gun-toting men who demanded her purse. Connie, solid as a rock, replied, "You don't want my purse, you want my money. I've got $ ---- ." She handed over the money, but she also looked them over, studied their car and memorized the license number.

When she eventually faced the two thugs in a courtroom, the judge praised her courage and follow-through, saying that "most women won't come to court to testify." Obviously, Connie is not "most women." She believed she was worth the time and trouble to hold her assailants responsible for their actions.

For most of us, though, standing firm and holding our ground is a reflex that is forged over time, not tested in a flash at gunpoint. In a letter from a woman who owns her own small business, that process comes to life:

"Sometimes I meet a 'newly' awakened woman just stepping into her assertiveness and I recognize the fury, frustration, and rage that are now history for me.

There is a mellowing... a softness ... Now when a man says he really believes men are better than women, I don't argue. I just laugh. Because the remark doesn't wound me as it used to.

When a vendor marvels at my business sense and my multiple-store operation and asks, 'You run all this by yourself? Such a little girl!' (I'm short.) I just smile.

What I'm trying to say is that I choose not to let outsiders hurt me .... sure, I still correct my live-in lover when he refers to the 'girls' in the office. But it is with firmness, not anger."

Knowing when and how to take a stand seems pretty easy, until that messy moment of truth arrives and shouts for action. Nancy faced just this sort of dilemma when she delivered the keynote address to an annual conference of one of the oldest and most respected professional medical associations in America. She says:

Exactly two minutes before I was to step onstage, an executive in a dark grey suit took me aside. A certain group of activist protesters intended to burst into the meeting and break up my presentation. If they did, I was supposed to remain calm, step to the back of the stage, and let the association president take over.

Well, I didn't feel very reassured. I was about to be thrust under bright lights before 3,000 people in a cavernous hall; I wanted to know what the fuss was about. The answer still rings in my head: "The Dalkon Shield", somebody said. The demonstrators objected to an award the association planned to give quietly, later in the week, to E. Claiborne Robins Sr., who had been chair of A.H. Robins when it sold its deadly contraceptive device.

The award was news to me, and it wasn't good: I was a Dalkon Shield claimant, one of 179,000 women and members of their families who say they've been damaged by the shield, plastic intrauterine contraceptive device. In the eyes of the claimants, E. Claiborne Robins Sr. headed the short list of responsible parties. I had a six-digit claim number and a forty-one-page claim form, facts I was sure the protesters had latched on to. Why else turn my speech into their platform?

All this careened through my head as I took the stage. I felt I had to go ahead with the keynote. I kept telling myself I wouldn't be endorsing their award by speaking, although I couldn't shake the sense that by living up to my professional contract, I would somehow be letting down all the claimants, myself included. What would the others have me do? Come clean, or keep my secret? Change my presentation right there and speak extemporaneously on corporate conscience gone bad? Stomp off the stage in disgust? As it turned out, no uninvited guests showed up, but during each minute of my speech, I kept wondering what I would do if they did.

To speak as planned was my decision, one I had to make in less than ninety seconds. You may not agree; I'm sure many readers are disappointed that I went ahead with it. You think I should have said something, given some sign that I was right and they were wrong. Of course all those sirens went off inside me when I heard about the award. In the end, what helped me the most was advice from a wise friend. "Follow your heart," she said. That I did.

Knowing that you are worth it means trusting that you can rescue yourself, stand firm, and feel great about acting in your own behalf. All of this can happen with the active support of friends and family, but don't delay if you find such support is scarce. Be the starter, the primary power to work positive changes for yourself, the assertive woman.

Suggested Reading

Courage is a Three Letter Word ... And That Word is YES by Walter Anderson. New York: Random House, 1986.

The Psychology of Self-Esteem by Nathaniel Branden. New York: Bantam Books, 1983.

Women and Self-Esteem: Understanding and Improving the Way We Think and Feel About Ourselves by Linda T. Sanford and Mary E. Donovan. New York: Penguin Books, 1985.

Chapter 11

Developing an Assertive Body Image

If truth is beauty, how come no one has their hair done in a library?
—— Lily Tomlin

Your body communicates as clearly as your words. Your style of emotional expression, posture, facial expressions, and voice quality are all tremendously important in becoming an assertive woman. This chapter will help you develop an assertive body image to make your body, as well as your words, communicate assertively.

A Body Image Inventory

Check yourself from head to toe, as you probably do frequently during the day, but this time measure yourself on a scale of assertiveness.

For example, women often have a problem making *eye contact* because many of us have been taught that it is more feminine to look away or look down. At times it can be coy to give little side glances and not to look directly at someone very long. In some cultures, it is considered disrespectful for women to make direct eye contact with men or authority figures. However, in our society, direct eye contact and holding your head erect is essential when you want to appear assertive and interested. This is not the same as staring at someone; look into the eyes, then perhaps look away for a few seconds or drop your gaze slightly so that you focus on the mouth of the person speaking to you. Practice making good eye contact with someone as you are talking and be aware of any differences in the quality of your communication. Are you listening better? Are you conveying more interest and receiving more attention to what you are saying?

What do your *facial expressions* say about you? Many women find it easy to smile and to demonstrate warmth, but when it comes to expressing anger or disapproval, they may do it with a smile. Use a mirror to see how you look when you are expressing anger, joy, sadness, fear, and other emotions. Get feedback from your friends, too. Practice making your face and head look assertive: make direct eye contact, feel the control over your facial muscles, and hold your head high.

While you are looking in the mirror, check out your *posture*. Changing your posture can change the way you feel about yourself. Try assuming a passive stance. Then change to an assertive stance ---- lean slightly forward with feet solidly grounded. Enjoy feeling centered with your body. Learn how close you like to stand or sit next to another person. This is your *optimal distance*. To find your optimal distance, stand across the room from a friend, face each other, and walk slowly toward your friend as she remains stationary. Make eye contact with her the whole way and then stop as soon as you feel that you have reached a comfortable distance from her. Measure this distance, and then have your friend repeat the process. You will discover that each person has her own optimal distance that aids assertion. If you can be aware of this fact with other people, it will help you to maintain an assertive posture. Assertiveness allows you to move toward a person, while passiveness involves hesitation, or moving away.

Next on your checklist for an assertive body image, notice your *gestures*. Do people say that you could not talk if someone tied your hands behind your back? If so, your gestures may be so distracting that they prevent you from delivering an assertive message. Or do you create a passive or indirectly aggressive image by holding your arms rigidly against your body, or folding them across your chest? Being able to move your hands and arms expansively demonstrates confidence and freedom. There are two kinds of gestures to practice. *Descriptive gestures* are those in which you practically paint a picture in the sky by sketching a scene or object in the air. Try this while describing your house to someone. Other gestures are *emphatic*. These underscore the significance of what you are saying, e.g., shaking your fist to show anger or pounding on a table to get someone's attention or putting your hand on someone's shoulder to connote caring and concern. Practice using emphatic gestures to show positive as well as negative feelings.

How are you dressed today? What sort of image do you convey by your *style of dress*? Everybody knows that dressing appropriately for a job interview increases your chances of getting the job. But do you realize that you can dress assertively too? Dressing in a favorite outfit can give you that extra touch of confidence to help you be assertive. Whenever you are feeling down, you can be assertive with yourself by wearing an outfit that doesn't let you fade into the woodwork — try wearing red — but attracts attention and helps you to project an outgoing appearance without being loud or coarse. Of course, style preferences vary. So, check out your own particular wardrobe and decide what your most assertive outfits are and use them as allies to help you.

There may be some special concerns you have about developing an assertive body image. For example, some overweight women have admitted to us that they have used their weight as a way to remain passive sexually or to avoid sex altogether. Similarly, women who are self-conscious about skin problems such as acne may be withdrawn and passive. Long after blemishes clear up, many women continue to see themselves as "acne-prone." At this point, an assertive attitude can be more helpful than losing weight or visiting a dermatologist.

Probably one of the most vital tools you can develop in becoming assertive is your *voice*. If you have a tape recorder or a friend to listen and give feedback, evaluate your voice in several different ways. Women, for the most part, seem to have higher-pitched but softer voices than men. However, for some, this is a conditioned tone rather than natural voice. In many instances Dorrie has tried to sound like a "baby doll" by raising the pitch of her voice, or Isabel has considered it feminine and sexy to "purr like a kitten." Unfortunately, these tones do not sound sincere, straightforward, or assertive, but are obvious distortions of what is natural. A lower-pitched voice is more often associated with assertion. Try to recite a poem in which you alternate raising and lowering your pitch to get a feeling for how you can vary and control your voice. When analyzing your voice, gauge its *volume*. Are you afraid to speak up for fear you will sound masculine? A woman can be loud and clear and still sound like a woman. It is better to be heard than to be disregarded. And yet, like Augusta, if you speak very loudly most of the time, you will risk turning people off.

Many times women give away the fact that they are nervous or anxious by speaking too rapidly. Your *rate of speech* needs to be evenly paced, not too fast or slow. Sometimes a slower rate is good in order to emphasize an important idea. Again, when angry, a woman may tend to talk very fast, trying to get it all said before she "runs out of steam." You can command someone's attention for a long time if you remember to use good eye contact and the other body elements we have mentioned. Also, *stressing* important words (usually nouns and verbs) can help you to sound assertive. Try emphasizing important words in a sentence, sometimes pausing before or after the word, by speaking key words louder, or by enunciating slowly and precisely.

Finally, you should be aware of the *quality* of your voice. Do you tend to whine when feeling helpless, powerless, or manipulative? Or, when nervous, does your voice become raspy and harsh? Practice asking for favors without whining. Try saying things that you are normally uncomfortable in saying, without a harsh, rasping tone. People will listen to and respect a full-bodied voice and tune out a squeaky, strident one.

You do not need a college education or a big vocabulary to be assertive and make yourself heard. If you practice the behaviors we have described and keep your messages simple, direct, and spontaneous, you will be on the way to becoming an assertive woman. In later chapters, we will offer specific suggestions to deal with particular situations where the content of what you say makes a big difference.

Reducing Anxiety and Promoting Relaxation

The assertive woman not only knows how to develop her body image, she knows how to promote her own physical well-being. There are many sources of information on healthful food habits and exercise. We assume these are available to you. Our concern is with more subtle body influences, especially nervousness and anxiety, which afflict many women.

Anxiety will detract from your assertive body image because it shows itself in your behavior. For most people, acting assertively in new situations evokes some initial anxiety and nervousness, which can be alleviated by learning to relax.

What happens to your body when you feel anxious? Headaches, a nervous stomach, asthma, and dizzy spells are common bodily indicators of anxiety. In more extreme forms, anxiety can be severe enough to be a contributing factor to ulcers, migraine headaches and heart attacks. In addition to the physical discomfort anxiety can produce, it can also cause emotional discomfort. Some people get cold feet and so avoid approaching employers for a raise in salary. Stage fright prevents many people from speaking in front of a group, even though the speech may have been interesting and valuable to the group; others clam up when they are treated unfairly and sacrifice their self respect in the process.

When facing threatening and anxiety provoking situations, Dorrie Doormat feels she has *no control* over her anxiety. Her anxiety immobilizes and controls her. Her anxiety is often at such a high level that she suffers severe headaches or fainting spells. She avoids anxiety-provoking situations because she feels powerless to do anything about them. The more she tries to avoid those anxiety-provoking situations, the stronger her anxiety becomes about facing them.

The assertive woman, in contrast, is not a helpless victim of anxiety; she alleviates it by taking action. By acting and therefore having control over what you do, you make it impossible for anxiety to control you. If you have felt that you couldn't tolerate a threatening situation ---- that your anxiety is so great that you really couldn't live through it ---- you have probably felt helpless to say or do anything. When you know that you can choose to assert yourself, you can live through threatening encounters and alleviate your anxiety because you can *benefit*, physically and/or emotionally, by saying or doing something ---- it doesn't have to be the perfect thing.

Learning to relax can combat anxiety and be a good complement to assertion. You may already practice forms of relaxation such as meditation, yoga, or a walk on the beach. While relaxation is not *necessary* for effective assertions, it can help you to feel more in control of your body.

You have probably noticed that you feel calmer and more relaxed after you have rested quietly even for a short time. By learning deep muscle relaxation, or another form of complete relaxation, you will be able to relax beyond this usual point. We recommend deep muscle relaxation as the easiest form to learn, but we also encourage you to explore other forms of relaxation. With practice you will be able to relax at will and counteract the tensions of anxiety arising from threatening situations.

We suggest that you practice deep muscle relaxation twice a day for one week. Be aware of particular muscle groups that are more difficult to relax than others, and give them special attention. For many people, the stomach, shoulders, and back are almost constantly tensed. When you have learned how to relax, you can practice relaxation together with acting assertively. Remember that you will alleviate your anxiety most effectively when you *act*.

To train yourself in deep muscle relaxation, choose a quiet, comfortable place where you won't be disturbed for half an hour. Go through a relaxation exercise while lying on the floor, a bed, or a reclining chair. Concentrate on each of the major muscle groups in your body, one at a time. Create tension in the muscles by tightening them for five seconds, then relax them. Practice this process of creating tension and achieving relaxation regularly, until you can become fully relaxed with a minimum of effort.

Detailed procedures for learning to relax by this method are offered in two of the books listed at the end of this chapter: *The Stress Owner's Manual* and *The Relaxation and Stress Reduction Workbook*.

Constructing Your Assertive Behavior Hierarchy

Dealing with tension and anxiety by relaxation is only a first step, although it is one that should be repeated as often as necessary. Your next step is to gain a better understanding of your sources of anxiety. What particular situations or encounters make you feel anxious? What causes you to be passive and non-assertive, causing you emotional and/or physical harm? What triggers your anger or aggression? It will be helpful for you to identify specific instances in which you would like to be more assertive. You can use an "assertive behavior hierarchy" to specify situations in which you find it difficult to assert yourself.

The hierarchies can be used individually or in a group to help identify each person's specific assertive deficits. Group time can be spent rehearsing the hierarchy items to minimize anxiety and learn assertive responses. Items are ordered according to the degree of anxiety produced by each situation, beginning with the least anxiety-provoking. Experiencing success with the first hierarchy items will encourage you to continue to practice assertive behaviors and responses as you face more demanding situations as an assertive woman.

Constructing and using your hierarchy will help you to become more aware of the specific times you behave non-assertively. It will also provide you with a starting point for the application of suggestions from this book to your own life.

It is important that you proceed through your hierarchy in order; resist the temptation to jump to the last items before you feel comfortable with the first ones. When you are comfortable asserting yourself with minor anxiety-provoking items, you'll find it much easier to proceed to the more difficult ones, and so increase the likelihood that you'll become an assertive woman.

Before completing your own hierarchy, review these examples:

DORRIE DOORMAT HIERARCHY

1. Returning that faulty toaster to the department store.

2. Initiating a conversation with my brother's new partner, Bill.

3. Asking not to be interrupted when Augusta starts talking in the middle of my conversation with Allison.

4. Cutting telephone calls short when I am busy, especially with Isabel and Augusta.

5. Asking questions of my car dealer without fear of sounding weak and stupid.

6. Giving a sincere compliment to my spouse or close friend.

7. Telling Allison when I have done something important or worthwhile.

8. Refusing unreasonable requests from my family, employer, and friends, especially Isabel Indirect and Augusta Aggressive.

9. Telling my spouse or close friend or relative that I disagree with an opinion he/she has expressed.

10. Expressing my anger to a very close relative or to my spouse in a non-apologetic way.

AUGUSTA AGGRESSIVE HIERARCHY

1. Complaining about poor restaurant service assertively, without name-calling.

2. Not interrupting Dorrie or Allison in the middle of a conversation.

3. In my classes, letting Dorrie and Isabel speak up without answering for them.

4. Listening to Allison criticize me for coming on too strong, without attacking her or being too defensive.

5. Not being overly critical of Dorrie because I know she won't fight back.

6. Expressing my positive feelings to Allison, Isabel, and Dorrie, by telling them when I appreciate something they have done.

7. Not bullying or shaming Dorrie into doing me a favor, knowing she'll be too guilty to say "no."

8. Being aware of another person's faults or vulnerabilities without teasing and making fun of her/him.

9. Talking about differences of opinion with my mate or close friend, not just saying "you're wrong."

10. Expressing anger without hitting, or throwing things, or being accusing or blaming.

ISABEL INDIRECT HIERARCHY

1. Asking Dorrie to drive me to work when my car is being repaired, without making her feel guilty if she can't drive me.

2. Give a compliment and approval openly and honestly, and not by using false flattery.

3. Being more direct when refusing door-to-door salespeople; not saying "my husband won't let me buy it."

4. Not making sarcastic or caustic comments about others behind their back.

5. Asking for something specific from my spouse without being dishonest and manipulative about why I want it.

6. When Augusta asks something unreasonable of me, saying "no" directly without becoming sullen and hostile.

7. Initiating the expression of love or affection with my mate without manipulating or being coy.

8. Expressing valid criticisms to my spouse honestly without resorting to indirect put-downs.

9. Asking for love and attention to be given to me without using guilt or manipulation to get it.

10. Expressing my anger openly to Dorrie, Augusta, or Allison by honestly stating that I am angry, instead of giving them the "silent treatment."

YOUR OWN ASSERTIVE BEHAVIOR HIERARCHY

Instructions: To construct your own hierarchy, select as the first item or situation something you feel you could handle assertively with only minimal anxiety. Continue to order your items from least anxiety-provoking to most anxiety-provoking. The last items should be the behaviors or situations that cause you the greatest anxiety and discomfort.

Suggested Reading

The Fountain of Age, by Betty Friedan. New York: Touchstone Books, 1994.

The Harvard Guide to Women's Health, by Karen Carlson, M.D., Stephanie Eisenstat, M.D., & Terra Ziporyn, Ph.D. Cambridge, MA: Harvard University Press, 1996.

The New Our Bodies, Ourselves, by The Boston Women's Health Book Collective. New York: Simon & Schuster, 1992.

The Relaxation and Stress Reduction Workbook (Fourth Edition), by Martha Davis, Matthew McKay, and Elizabeth Robbins Eshelman. Richmond, California: New Harbinger Publications, 1995.

The Stress Owner's Manual: Meaning, Balance and Health in Your Life, by Ed Boenisch and Michele Haney. San Luis Obispo, California: Impact Publishers, 1996.

Talking from 9 to 5: Women and Men in the Workplace: Language, Sex, and Power, by Deborah Tannen. New York: Avon Books, 1995.

You Just Don't Understand: Women and Men in Conversation, by Deborah Tannen. New York: Ballantine Books, 1991.

Chapter 12

Compliments, Criticism, and Rejection

I have a fear of being disliked, even by people I dislike.
—— Oprah Winfrey

How do you feel about compliments?

A genuine compliment is a specific expression of appreciation, sincerely given. But we don't have too look far to find imitations. Compliments —— not always sincere —— run rampant in the Compassion Trap, when we compulsively praise others in an attempt to make them feel good —— even at our own expense. Because the Compassion Trap is a prominent feature of so many women's lives, it is easy to find women who overuse compliments as a way to compensate for unacceptable negative feelings about a friend, spouse, or employer. They search for an elusive silver lining in a sky full of dark clouds, and thus avoid having to acknowledge the clouds at all. It's positive thinking gone bad.

Then there is false flattery. Women are often expected to be easy prey to flattery because, supposedly, they require constant reassurance and will respond to tiny, frivolous attentions. Just a little buttering up, and she'll go along without complaint. Bring the underpaid secretary a bouquet and she'll be dissuaded from pressing for that raise. Avoid helping her paint the living room by remarking how extremely talented she is at these things. Instead of giving her the sweater she really wants for her birthday, buy her a new blender, and tell her how glad you are she isn't selfish and self-centered like most women.

Fortunately, neither women nor men are born to be flattered! Learn to give and acknowledge genuine compliments, and along the way discover when a different approach is better.

• A woman who works closely with you is going through a messy divorce. She looks haggard and depressed. Instead of chirping "Oh, Tracy, don't you look wonderful?" in a well-intentioned effort to cheer her up, you might instead say: "Tracy, are you free for lunch? I know you're having a rough time, and I'd like to help if I can."

• You are redecorating your home, and have been working with an interior designer who comes highly recommended. After several weeks of work, the designer excitedly submits her plans. One look is enough to tell you that it's all wrong. Rather than search for the one tiny element that you *do* like ("This pillow fabric is nice!"), take the plunge: "Carol, I can see you have knocked yourself out on this project, and I appreciate it very much. The only trouble is that this isn't what I had in mind. Let's go over it and see how it could be changed. First, I prefer stripes to polka dots for the chairs ...."

What Gets in the Way: Embarrassment and Fear

Even when compliments are genuine and sincere, they make many women (and men) uncomfortable. Many of us believe that it is embarrassing, unladylike, impolite, or just plain bad manners to acknowledge a compliment. Instead, we argue or reject what is said ("Oh, come on! Are you kidding? Give me a break!"). The response usually succeeds: the complimenter, having said the wrong thing, won't risk repeating the error.

If you feel uncomfortable when you give or receive a compliment, review the list below. Which match your own reactions?

* I tend to blush when complimented and it embarrasses me.
* A compliment paves the way for the real point — something unpleasant or critical.
* Other people may think I deserve a compliment, but I know better. You can't kid a kidder.
* I don't like being the center of attention. I never know how to react.
* Giving a compliment is simply a request to receive one in return.
* Compliments are thinly disguised attempts to conceal the true motives of the complimenter; I don't trust them.
* Saying "thank you" without argument sounds conceited.

* I don't need compliments; I know my own worth.
* Compliments make me very nervous.
* I can't live up to a compliment.
* I'm too shy.
* If I worked up the courage to give someone a compliment and then she or he laughed at me, I'd die.
* Giving compliments is unnecessary; the people I would want to compliment know what they're good at already.

If any of these reasons sound familiar to you, is it because you feel obligated to give a compliment in return for one? You certainly don't have to reciprocate with a compliment, but do acknowledge what was said. It can be done verbally or nonverbally, with a smile or a nod of the head. If you want to say something, "thank you" is simple, elegant, and enough. You may also add a word or two about how you feel about what was said to you: "Allison, I really admire the way you said 'no' to that car salesman. You didn't beat around the bush" The assertive reply: "Thanks, Linda. It has taken me a while to learn how to say "no' assertively, and I am really beginning to feel confident. I'm glad you noticed!"

Developing Confidence in Compliments

Use this checklist to develop your ability to give and receive compliments. As you master each item, check it off the list.

* Don't fall into the Compassion Trap by giving inappropriate compliments or false flattery in an attempt to make someone feel good.
* Do give sincere compliments as expressions of your appreciation.
* Do make your compliment specific.
* Do acknowledge a compliment you receive, either verbally or non-verbally.
* Don't feel embarrassed or put down by a genuine compliment.
* Don't feel obligated to give a compliment in return for one.
* Don't use good news as a way to ease into the bad news.

Criticism

Any inhibition we experience giving and receiving compliments is heightened in giving criticism. Probably the prime fear that keeps many women from giving or accepting criticism is the fear of rejection. When your self-esteem is low, or the situation is especially sensitive, it doesn't take too much to paralyze you with anxiety and fear at the moment of delivering or receiving critical remarks. As your confidence grows, your ability to evaluate criticism objectively will also.

When you are as non-assertive as Dorrie, you tend to evaluate what people say to you, or what you say, in terms of your own feelings of worthlessness. However, when you are assertive like Allison, your self-image remains strong and intact; you can acknowledge your own faults without feeling rejected by others. In fact, being assertive in giving and receiving criticism will earn you respect, and people will turn toward you rather than away.

One reason criticism can be hard to hear is the element of surprise. Usually the criticism that is least expected is the one that stings. To overcome the fear of criticism, then, set up a step-by-step process that will gradually desensitize you to critical remarks, whether anticipated or not.

Prepare in advance for three possible types of criticism: unrealistic criticism, put-downs, and valid criticism. Be careful not to over-prepare or to feel that you must be constantly on guard.

Unrealistic criticism is the sort that is utterly ridiculous, e.g. Augusta calling a slim person a "big, fat slob." Put-downs may have an element of truth, but are said in a patronizing and/or insulting way, such as Isabel saying to someone who is overweight, "Why don't you have a banana split? You'll never notice a few more pounds!"

Valid criticism is both realistic and stated in a straightforward, assertive manner, such as Allison saying to an overweight friend, "I have noticed that you have gained some extra weight. I think you really looked better and healthier before."

CHECK YOUR C.Q. (CRITICISM QUOTIENT)

Use our checklist to determine how sensitive you are to criticism. Put a "plus" (+) by those that you handle assertively, a "minus" (-) by those that you avoid handling at all, and a check (✓) by those that you face but handle awkwardly. Your ratings here will be important to the exercise on criticism at the end of the chapter.

_____ Someone criticizes you about a fault that you cannot deny is yours.

_____ You give a friend an honest criticism of what you see as a legitimate problem.

_____ Someone criticizes you for an act that you know without a doubt doesn't apply to you and is ridiculous.

_____ Someone has put you down in an indirect way; there may be some truth to the put-down, but it's basically unfair.

_____ Things have not been going your way lately and you are lacking confidence. You're criticized for "being down."

_____ You have just gained the courage to give a friend a valid criticism.

_____ Your friend cannot handle this and retaliates by criticizing you with a mixture of valid and invalid complaints.

_____ You are feeling very happy and high spirited. Someone not so happy is jealous and tries to bring you down by reminding you of things she knows can hurt your feelings.

Rejection

Everyone wants to avoid being rejected as a person, but you can't avoid having your ideas or behavior rejected. The most common form of rejection occurs when someone says "no" to your idea, request, or action. Becoming assertive means learning to accept a "no" as meaning "no" to the situation at hand, instead of interpreting it as total rejection. Nevertheless, it is possible that the other person may wish to convey that you are worthless. But, if you feel good about yourself, you will not accept this interpretation. You'll be able to accept some "no's," because your reward is primarily in asserting yourself, not just in getting what you want.

A REJECTION CHECKLIST

Use the following checklist to determine in what ways you may fear rejection. Put a check (✓) in front of each item that causes you to feel rejected regardless of its truth. Put a plus (+) before each item that you can handle assertively.

_____ Your parents, spouse, or boss tells you that you are stupid and can't do anything right.

_____ Your lover criticizes your appearance.

_____ A friend says she or he is busy and cannot go with you someplace you wanted to go.

_____ Your child or another's child tells you that you're mean and that she/he hates you.

_____ Someone whose intelligence you respect tells you that your latest brainstorm isn't a good idea.

_____ You're playing a game where sides are chosen by leaders --- you're last to be picked.

_____ In a group, you make an important statement which is ignored.

_____ You have completed a job as well as you can, but you are told to do it over.

_____ You look for physical affection from someone you love who is too busy to give it to you at the moment.

_____ You have asked someone to do a special favor for you, and she refuses.

_____ A significant person in your life forgets your birthday or anniversary.

_____ You apply for a job or admission to a certain school or organization, and are turned down.

Review the items that cause you to feel anxious and fearful about rejection. If you feel discouraged about the way you answered, the first exercise below will be a good antidote.

Action Exercises

LIKE YOURSELF FIRST

Write down ten positive statements about yourself --- things you like about *you* as a person: "I like the fact that I'm trying to become a more assertive person." Stand in front of a mirror and read each item on your list aloud. While practicing good eye contact and smiling appropriately, acknowledge each compliment that you give yourself either verbally or non-verbally. Practice adding some free information to some of your "thank-you's."

Use this list to gain confidence. Refer to it often and add to it by telling someone, in regular conversation, something positive about yourself.

GIVING AND RECEIVING COMPLIMENTS

Try giving and receiving compliments with a friend. If you try this in a group, have each woman turn to the woman on her right to give her a compliment. After the woman acknowledges the compliment, continue around the circle until you are all feeling comfortable with both giving and receiving. Be sure to give each other feedback: first, on positives about the way in which compliments are delivered or received; then, give each other specific suggestions for improvement that might be necessary.

GIVING AND RECEIVING CRITICISM

Take at least fifteen minutes and write two separate lists with five to ten items on each list. Title the first list "Unrealistic Criticisms" and write down what you feel would be ridiculous criticisms of yourself. On the second list, "Realistic Criticisms," write down things that you feel are valid criticisms of yourself. Then exchange both lists with another person and take turns reading to one another from your lists, alternating preposterous and realistic items while being as believable and dramatic as possible.

Whenever you are confronted with an unrealistic criticism, contradict it openly, as in the following example:

"WHY DON'T YOU TRY SOCIAL WORK?"

School counselor: "Allison, I think your decision to become a psychiatrist is impractical. You aren't good at science and math, you know. Why don't you try social work?"

Allison: "That is not true. My aptitudes in math and science are very strong, and I think becoming a psychiatrist is a practical goal for me."

On the other hand, when responding to a *realistic criticism*, the assertive woman will acknowledge the criticism as valid and then may add a statement about how she is working on that problem and is trying to change. Or, she may say that she is aware that a trait bothers others, but that it doesn't bother her and she's really not motivated to do anything about it now. For example, Allison's reply to her school counselor might sound like this:

Allison: "You're right about science and math not being my strongest subjects. However, I've arranged for individual tutoring and plan to master those subjects. I will do whatever I can to make sure I can reach my goal of becoming a psychiatrist."

HANDLING PUT-DOWNS

Few topics in this book have generated as much animated discussion as this one! There are several ways to handle a put-down: ignore it; respond with a direct assertive statement; respond in kind with a rapid-fire, witty retort.

Ignore it. This is often the most effective choice. We don't suggest that you walk off in a huff, working up a head of steam all the while. If you choose this option, it means you literally let the remark pass. You may, of course, add a little touch of your own, as a friend did. A sales rep from an audio-visual equipment company was demonstrating a new slide projector to the support staff in her office. At one point in the demonstration, the rep said to Cynthia, "This projector is so easy to disassemble that even you could do it." Cynthia's reaction? She broke up laughing! Without saying a word, she responded from strength and confidence, making the put-down small and petty, not herself. (The rep didn't get that order, either.)

Respond with a direct assertive statement. Some put-downs are part of a pattern which must be addressed. Kathleen's boss, for example, consistently patronized her by following every request with "There's a good girl," a remark that made Kathleen's blood boil. Ignoring it was impossible. The next time her boss uttered those four words, Kathleen said: "Please don't call me a 'good girl.' It's irritating." She made her point assertively and although she found she had to repeat it several times, she reports that it was an effective way to handle the problem.

Respond in kind with a witty retort. In the first edition of *The Assertive Woman,* this topic was chock full of quick, razor-sharp retorts to some popular put-downs. In this edition, we give less attention to this approach because it was not particularly successful for many women who tried it. Although it was always a favorite exercise in seminars ---- and we still recommend it as a way to discover there are alternatives to freezing up ---- in real life, women found it a sometimes reckless response. In the hands of Rosie O'Donnell, a witty retort works beautifully; but for most of us, it's better to find a response that we can live with. (One we still like: "You did a great job, considering you're a woman." Response: "For a man, you didn't do too bad, either.") There is nothing wrong with practicing a quick retort to give you a feeling of control. Our advice, however, is: *handle with care!* The objective is to hold on to your sense of worth, not to attack.

If witty retorts aren't your style, you can always respond to a put-down directly and assertively. Saying "I'm offended by that remark," or a similar statement of feeling can be just as potent. If a sense of humor is one of your characteristics, you might discover a new application for it here (we take a closer look at it in Chapter 17, "Humor"). In the meantime, record the put-downs you've received or heard, and see if you can come up with some effective retorts ---- either funny or direct. This exercise is, as you might imagine, a lot of fun to work on in a group!

MAKING FRIENDS WITH MS. PROTECTO

Here is a group exercise which will help you to reduce anxiety about giving compliments and criticisms, and aid you in being more spontaneous and open. It involves getting rid of the censor inside your head (Ms. Protecto), which tells you to be overly cautious and not risk saying the wrong thing.

Have one person stand before each person in the group one-by-one and quickly blurt out a few adjectives and nouns ---- positive and negative ---- that describe what she notices about each person. Stay away from phrases and sentences and just use one-worders. Move quickly from person to person and have each person take a turn. For example, you may look at a person and say, "short, warm smile, fuzzy, serious, unpredictable, bald, plump, caring, social, bright colors, fifty-ish." The person being spoken to remains neutral and does not comment on anything said about her. Have each person try this until she feels she can be spontaneous with her remarks.

Then think about how comfortable or uncomfortable this exercise was for you. It's even better if you can talk about it with someone. Be specific about what types of words cause you the most trouble ---- negative or positive or both. Try this exercise again until you feel that you have reached a level of spontaneity that is right for you.

ACCEPTING "NO" FOR AN ANSWER

Make a list with three columns: *who, what* and *when*. Under "who" write down the names of people whose rejection you are sensitive about. Under "what" list specific situations in which you feel most vulnerable to a "no" response. And finally under "when" write down the times in which you feel most threatened by hearing a "no." Then order these, putting the ones that cause you the least anxiety on top of the list as #1, and continue numbering until you end with the most threatening who, what, and when at the bottom.

Sample:

Who	What	When
children	asking for help around the house	at home at dinnertime
employer	asking for time off	at work during a hectic day
friend	expecting company	chores have piled up around the house
husband	making love	when feeling down
other(s)	other(s)	other(s)

Now that you have the samples to go on, make up your own lists, ordering them from the least anxiety provoking to the most threatening.

When you have completed and ordered your list, role-play these situations with a friend or in a group starting with the first item in each column. Practice until you feel comfortable with hearing a "no" from your partner. Then move on to the next. Each time you hear a "no" think to yourself, "I am okay for making this request. I am not being rejected as a person; only my *request* is being rejected. I can make this request at another time, and it may be accepted. I feel good about asserting myself and expressing my needs clearly."

Chapter 13

Saying "No"

The Queen turned crimson with fury, and after glaring at [Alice] for a moment like a wild beast, began screaming, "Off with her head! Off with —"
"Nonsense!" said Alice, and the Queen was silent.

— Lewis Carroll
Alice in Wonderland

Being "feminine" has often meant that a woman was submissive and indecisive, and that when she said "no" she *really* meant "yes!" It is hardly surprising that women found it a struggle to say no. Since women continuously encounter requests from others to do something for them or advertisements insisting that they buy, it is an enormous handicap not to know how to refuse.

Women have made great strides over the last ten years, but it's still not so easy to say no. One of the biggest barriers to saying no is the Compassion Trap — the drive to take care of someone else's needs in spite of your own (described in Chapter 7). For Dorrie, it is better to say "yes" than to deal with the guilt she likely feels after an assertive refusal. Or, she may resist the idea that she has the right to evaluate a situation herself and the right to disagree.

Dorrie lacks confidence in her own decision-making power. She feels worthless next to others, and believes that their needs are naturally more important. Like Dorrie, some women say yes to avoid conflict. Others fear that refusal can lead to violence. Some young girls, in fact, have unwisely agreed to meet men they've only communicated with over the Internet, even though they've been expressly warned against such meetings.

Four Ways to Say "No"

One of the toughest hurdles to overcome is to decide whether the other person's request of you is reasonable. Don't look to the other person to see if the request is reasonable; the simple fact that the request was made means that the person has decided that she/he wants you to comply, regardless. Look inside yourself first: If you hesitate or hedge, or if you feel cornered or trapped, or you notice a tightness or nervousness in your body, it may mean that the request in unreasonable. Sometimes you may be genuinely confused or unsure because you just do not have enough information to know for sure.

Next, assert your right to ask for more information. Many of us grew up under the influence of such dicta as "Children should be seen and not heard," or under religious dogma that could not be challenged. Nevertheless, the first step in asserting yourself when a request is made of you is to make sure you have all the facts. Allison does not commit herself to a yes or no until she fully understands what is being asked of her.

Third, practice saying "no." Once you understand the request and decide you do not want to do it or buy it, say so firmly and calmly. It is crucial that you give a simple "no," not a complicated statement filled with excuses, justifications, and rationalizations. It is enough that you do not want to do this simply because you do not want to do it. You can accompany your refusal with a simple, straightforward explanation of what you are feeling. A direct explanation is assertive; indirect and misleading excuses are non-assertive and can get you into a lot of trouble by leaving you open for further challenge.

Finally, learn to say no without saying "I'm sorry, but ...." Saying "I'm sorry" weakens your stand, and another person, especially Isabel, will play on your guilt. When you evaluate a situation carefully and decide the best thing is to say no, you have nothing to be sorry about. Allison feels strong and happy with her decisions to say no.

The Broken Record

When an aggressive person like Augusta does not accept your assertive refusal and applies high-pressure tactics, you can use the so-called "broken record" method. You simply become a "broken record" and repeat your original assertive refusal each time Augusta tries another tactic to push you to change your mind. If you stand firm with your original statement, and resist the temptation to answer "Why?" or respond to insults, she will soon run out of new material and give up. If you tire before this happens, you can end the conversation or change the topic. *Watch out for this technique, however; it can be hard on relationships!*

"YOU WON'T MIND, WILL YOU?"

Imagine the following scenario: A close friend has three small children. She has frequently called on you to watch them for a couple of hours at a time, since she is in real estate part-time and has to see clients at a minute's notice and at odd hours. You are home anyway, so she assumes you won't mind watching them. However, she has gotten tied up lately and two hours drag on for six or seven. You cannot reach her by phone and so you can't do what you have to do. She calls you on the day you have set aside to clean out your garage and prepare for a garage sale. What would you do? Let's see how Allison would handle it.

Jan: "Oh, Allison, I really have a big buyer today. This one could get me out of debt. You won't mind watching my children for a while, would you?"

Allison: "What do you mean by 'a while'? How long will you be away?"

Jan: "Oh, I don't know exactly. This is a hot one though, and it shouldn't take more than an hour or two."

Allison: "Let me think a moment.... Lately, Jan, when I have watched the kids, you have gotten tied up for longer than you expected and I have no way to reach you. I really cannot risk being tied up with the kids today, and I will have to say no."

Jan: "Allison, what can I say? I need your help to make this sale."

Allison: "I really have to say no, Jan."

Jan: "Well, I suppose I could call a sitter."

Allison: "That would be great! I'm glad you understand. Let me know whether or not you close the deal."

Exercising your *right to refuse* and giving yourself *time to evaluate requests* are both active ways to protect your resources. Any valuable resource, when drawn upon frequently, will become depleted. When that resource is your energy, time, or love, knowing how to protect it is vitally important to your happiness.

"ENOUGH IS ENOUGH."

Kim, a college student, was an active participant in several major campus organizations. She maintained a high scholastic average and spent several hours each day studying before attending one of her many meetings. Kim's reputation as a natural leader grew along with her list of organization meetings and appointments. She didn't want to drop any of her activities, even though she frequently felt too tired to enjoy an evening out with friends. After one particularly exhausting week, Kim decided to see a doctor for a routine check-up. She had mononucleosis, and as a result she was instructed to withdraw from college for the semester to have complete rest. For Kim, trying to do too much resulted in not being able to do anything at all.

Beth is a talented photographer who enjoys her work. She encountered such enthusiastic demand for her services that she spent every minute trying to satisfy all of the requests for her time. She didn't want to refuse anyone because she really loved photography. But Beth's talent also became her liability as her schedule grew heavier and heavier, and her free time was swallowed up. Wisely, Beth refused some photography assignments, worked to stabilize her schedule, and successfully protected her talent and her enjoyment.

Giving yourself time to evaluate requests made of you will also protect your resources. You don't have to commit yourself to something as soon as you are asked to do it. "Let me think it over and get back to you" is an important statement to make.

Before you make your decision, ask yourself:

* Do I really want to do this, or am I only trying to please someone else?
* What will I receive for my participation?
* If I decide to do this, will it continue to be rewarding or will it become oppressive?

"No" Without Guilt

For many women, saying no produces guilt, regardless of the appropriateness of the refusal. The following situations show you how saying no can be an effective ---- and guilt-free ---- process. Imagine yourself in the situations as you read them, and practice feeling good about saying no. As we have noted before, real life situations will not always go this smoothly, but these examples help illustrate an assertive approach.

"MY CAR IS IN THE SHOP"

Carol has taken her car into the shop for repairs. The mechanic gave her an estimate of $55. When she returns to pick up her car, Carol is told that the repairs come to $110. She asks to see the shop manager, and tells her/him that the price is much higher than the estimate that she was given, and that she feels the higher charges are not justified. The manager begins a lengthy description of all repairs performed on her car. Carol listens carefully, and replies that she still believes the charges are excessive. She adds that she will contact the Automotive Repair Board to complain, and that she won't be bringing her car to this shop in the future. The manager consults with the mechanic and upon her/his return, concedes that the mechanic had made an error in the computation, and the charges will be $55. Carol pays the charges and resolves to find a more trustworthy repair shop.

"IT'S NOT QUITE WHAT I WANT"

Debbie has been shopping for a sturdy bookcase. At a large department store, she asks the salesperson to show her several bookcases. None of them are quite right. Debbie tells the salesperson that she doesn't think any of them will work out, and the salesperson takes her to another section of the store where there are several more models. After disassembling one of them to demonstrate how sturdily built it is, the salesperson asks Debbie if she doesn't think it would do. Debbie appreciates the time and effort the salesperson took to show her the bookcases, but she has not found what she wanted. She thanks the salesperson for all the help, and tells him that the bookcases aren't quite what she had in mind. She leaves the store, glad that she didn't buy something that she really didn't like, despite the salesperson's extra effort.

"WOULD YOU STAY WITH THE KIDS TONIGHT?"

Kay's parents ask that she do quite a bit of babysitting for her brothers and sisters. Her parents are very active, and Kay often babysits four or five nights a week. As a result, Kay missed out on social activities with her friends. Kay has tried sulking and moping around the house, without success. She decides to try to explain her feelings to her parents and reach some kind of compromise. When she does, her parents are surprised and indignant. Kay repeats her feelings calmly, explaining the situation and emphasizing that she would very much like to participate in some social activities of her own. She adds that she would be happy to babysit once or twice a week, but babysitting four or five times a week is really unreasonable. Her parents feel that her solution is a good one and they agree to get another babysitter for other times. Kay does not feel that she has let her parents down.

"BUT WHAT ABOUT GRANDPA?"

Suzanne's eighty-year-old grandfather has been bedridden for several months. Suzanne is particularly fond of him, and she often seeks his advice. Recently, however, he has been demanding to see Suzanne more and more often and asking her to read to him for several hours at a time.

Suzanne wants to comfort her grandfather in whatever ways she can, but his requests are interfering with her other activities. She doesn't want to hurt her grandfather's feelings, but she feels she must find a better way to handle the situation. She discusses the problem with her friends and family, explains her other responsibilities and asks each of them to set aside a little time each day to read to her grandfather. She meets some resistance, but finds a sister and cousin who are happy to help and she is able to work out a schedule that is manageable for everyone.

"TOO MUCH TOO SOON"

Julie's new boyfriend, Tom, has recently begun pressuring her to have sex. Julie truly cares for Tom, and wants the relationship to work, but she's not ready to have sex with him.

Tom: "You know, Julie, we've been going out for almost two months now, and I really want to make love to you. But every time I get close to you, you push me away... I thought we had something going here."

Julie: "I think we do have 'something going,' Tom, but my divorce is barely final. I just know that I'm not comfortable with starting a physical relationship right now. I need you to respect that."

Julie knows that sex is an extremely personal issue. Tom does not have the right to force or coerce her into having sex or participating in sexual activities that she's uncomfortable with. Her health and safety are paramount; learning to say no in this day and age is crucial. (See "Sexuality and Safety" in Chapter 15.)

A Resource Checklist

The first step in protecting your resources and making your strengths work *for* you is identifying what personal strengths *you* have and want to preserve. Check as many as apply to you.

* What do you spend a large part of your time doing?

___ cooking, laundry
_✓_ studying, reading
_✓_ working away from home
___ driving
___ attending school
___ caring for children, family members
___ pursuing hobby (photography, writing, etc.)
_✓_ watching TV, movies
___ entertaining
___ other

* What specific requests are regularly made of you?

___ driving
___ doing errands
_✓_ working overtime
___ attending meetings, accepting leadership positions
___ talking with friends, counseling friends
___ donating time or volunteering for worthy causes
___ travelling
___ other

* What tasks or situations do your family and friends frequently call on you to help with?

___ planning social events ⏤ birthdays, etc.
___ cooking and/or housecleaning
___ chauffeuring
_✓_ watching the children
___ loaning money
_✓_ visiting and caring for relatives
___ other

* If you feel proficient in certain areas, do you leave yourself enough time to enjoy "doing your thing"?

Give some thought to these questions and identify the resources you have by looking closely at your answers. They will give you an idea of the resources you draw upon often and need to protect.

The assertive woman can say "no" to requests when she is already busy, and she can give herself time to decide what she will do. By exercising these two options, she protects her strengths and prevents them from becoming her liabilities.

Suggested Reading

Don't Say YES When You Want to Say NO by Herbert Fensterheim, Ph.D., and Jean Baer. New York: Dell, 1975.

Learning to Say No: Establishing Healthy Boundaries by Carla Wills-Brandon, M.A. Deerfield Beach, Florida: Health Communications, Inc., 1990.

Chapter 14

Manipulation

Women have the same desires as men, but do not have the same right to express them.

---- Jean Jacques Rousseau

One of the splendid things about an assertive woman is that she'll tell it to you straight. She's not a game player, and you don't need a magic decoder ring to figure out what's on her mind. Unfortunately, however, there must still be a lot of women who will stoop to deception or trickery to get what they want (until this strategy blows up in their faces, and it always does, eventually).

That's the only explanation we can think of for the current craze for a silly volume of feminine do's and don'ts cleverly titled *The Rules*. Authors Ellen Fein and Sherrie Schneider hand down (from a grandmother, no less, who had "more proposals than shoes") 35 "time-tested secrets for capturing the heart of Mr. Right." Obeying "The Rules," they say, is simple: "In plain language, we're talking about playing hard to get!" Not exactly what we'd call an honest beginning to a relationship.

All the same, women have taken this little book to heart. Maybe it's because grandma's shoe is on the other foot: women have always known what it's like to be targets for classic manipulative behavior, pressed to do another's bidding through the skillful use of guilt, shame, or an overpowering sense of duty. Now, women make "The Rules," but these, alas, are the wrong ones.

We define manipulation as the deliberate or unconscious use of indirect and dishonest means to achieve a desired goal. Let's face it, such sneaky behavior can be persuasive, but it only succeeds when you respond to the hidden part of the message. Assertiveness is refreshingly honest and straightforward; what you see is what you get. A manipulator can be very good at getting what she wants while appearing to do nothing at all; she loads what she says with guilt or shame to make you feel you have no choice but to do as she wishes. An assertive woman acts for herself; she does not choose for others.

For a peek at manipulation in action, consider this scenario:

THE 2-FOR-1 ROOMMATE

Dorrie, a young working woman, has taken on a roommate to help with day-to-day living expenses. She likes Isabel, but is getting tired of Isabel's boyfriend, Irv, who spends even more time in the apartment than Isabel does. One of the reasons Dorrie chose Isabel as her roommate in the first place was that they worked different hours, and Dorrie would have the apartment to herself while Isabel was away at work.

Instead, here's Irv, eating, sleeping, and hanging around the apartment most of the day. Finally, Dorrie decides to talk to Isabel about the situation.

Dorrie: "Isabel, I'm sorry to have to bring this up, but Irv spends more time here than you do. I really wish he'd find his own place."

Isabel: "Gee, I thought you liked him --- he sure likes you, you know. And he is looking for work, but nobody appreciates his talent enough to hire him."

Dorrie: "Oh, I like him, it's not that, it's just that I wanted to have time to myself during the day, and now he's always around..."

Isabel: "Aren't you being a tad selfish? Sometimes you have to think of other people, too, Dorrie. I'm telling you as a friend. Irv's a good guy and he's doing the best he can. If you can't understand that ..."

Dorrie: "No, no, I see. Forgive me. I didn't mean to offend you. Of course I don't want to inconvenience Irv, or you, either. Let's just forget about it."

No contest: Irv sticks around and Dorrie feels guilty and ashamed that raw self-interest could make her so insensitive. Isabel correctly assumed that arousing guilt would be the easiest way to keep Irv and the apartment, as well as control over her hapless roommate. After a day or so, Dorrie only feels resentment and anger.

THE 2-FOR-1 ROOMMATE, TAKE 2

Suppose that Dorrie handled the same encounter assertively. Notice the difference between manipulation and persistent assertion:

Dorrie: "Isabel, I'd like to talk with you about Irv spending so much time here. I'm glad to have you as my roommate, and I think that can continue if we set some reasonable limits. I'm uneasy that Irv is here so much."

Isabel: "What, you want to throw him out on the street? That doesn't sound like you, Dorrie. I thought you liked him."

Dorrie: "It's time to set reasonable limits that are fair to both of us. You are my roommate and you pay half the rent; that was the arrangement, and it suited both of us. But I don't want two roommates."

Isabel: "A little oversensitive, aren't you, Dorrie? Irv doesn't live here, really, and anyway, it's only for a little while longer, when he gets on his feet. Maybe you've never been in a tight spot before, but you need friends at a time like this..."

Dorrie: "Isabel, the fact is that I'm uncomfortable with the situation as it is and I want it to change. Either we agree that Irv will only be here when you are, or we part company."

Isabel: "Okay, I get the picture. I'll talk to Irv, but I don't think he's going to go for that. So, thanks to you, I'll have to move again, as if I have time."

Dorrie: "Thanks for agreeing to talk with him. I think that's the best solution."

In this version, Dorrie effectively and assertively confronted Isabel. She didn't allow herself to get sidetracked by Isabel's attempts to make her feel guilty or responsible. They may not be lifelong friends, but they both learned a lesson.

Emotional Blackmail

Emotional blackmail is manipulation at its most powerful. The emotional blackmailer, consciously or unconsciously, is able to coerce a victim into a particular action by playing on the victim's compassion, fear or guilt. Emotional blackmailers, as well as other manipulators, find ideal targets in women trapped by compassion. Because compulsively compassionate women place others' wishes and feelings ahead of their own, they are easily exploited, and can be made to feel guilty simply for thinking of their own feelings and needs.

Emotional blackmail can only take place under certain conditions. Typically, it involves two people who have established a close personal or intimate relationship (mother and daughter; husband and wife; sister and sister; two close friends). Note, however, that just because you have a close relationship with someone does not mean you will end up as a blackmailer or victim!

This is how it works: once a close relationship has been established, the blackmailer will interact with the victim in the best, and sometimes the only way she/he knows: through indirect manipulation. The victim must care for or love the blackmailer. The blackmailer always has something the victim wants — usually love or attention. The blackmailer can coerce the victim into a particular action (or prevent the victim from doing something) by capitalizing on the victim's emotions.

As with other forms of manipulation, emotional blackmail only works if the victim colludes with the blackmailer. The victim will remain trapped as long as she fears the consequences of escaping. In most cases, she stays because she's afraid of losing the blackmailer's love.

The following examples of emotional blackmail illustrate the subtlety of the manipulative process.

HER NIGHT OUT

Scenario: A woman is getting ready to meet four women friends for dinner, when her husband tells her he thinks a night out with pals is fine, but: "You tell them everything! I'm always the bad guy. I wonder if you really value our relationship, since you gossip all night. I just want you to know that if I leave, I'm not the one to blame."

Result: The woman (victim) feels compelled to cancel her dinner plans to keep the peace.

The would-be blackmailer could have taken an assertive approach by saying, "I'm upset about your spending so much time with friends because I feel left out."

LETTER OF RECOMMENDATION

Scenario: Two close friends are discussing the difficulty of getting a good job in their field. Isabel has a lead on a job opening, and has asked Allison if she would submit a letter of recommendation to the prospective employer. Allison doesn't feel she can write an informative letter because she has never worked with Isabel and knows nothing specific about Isabel's skills. Isabel pleads with Allison to write the letter anyway: "Look, we've been friends for a long time. You know me better than anyone. If you were *really* my friend, you'd write the letter. If you really cared, you'd do it."

Result: Allison (victim) decides to write the letter for Isabel (blackmailer) to save the friendship.

A more honest and assertive message from Isabel could be: "I'm afraid you won't write the letter for me, and I really need your help."

"DON'T BE TOO FRIENDLY"

Scenario: A man and woman are on their way to a dinner party, where they will see quite a few mutual friends. As they drive, he says, "You know, it would be smart if you didn't say too much to John tonight. He's a friend, and I like him, but his divorce has only been final for a couple of months. If you spend a lot of time around him, people are bound to wonder what's going on, especially with you in that dress."

Result: She (victim) agrees she'll avoid John as much as possible (collusion), since she certainly wouldn't want to make a fool of herself or upset the man (blackmailer) who escorted her to the party.

A better way for him to tell her what's on his mind:

"You know, you're a lovely, intelligent woman, and I know everyone who'll be at the party agrees with me. Just don't forget about me, okay?"

Everyone, at some time, may be tempted to try a hand at blackmail or manipulation. But the indirect approach is very costly: it can destroy people and the bonds between them, and there is no way to repair the damage.

The Question Trap

Before you can deal effectively with manipulation, you have to be able to recognize it when it happens. One manipulative strategy is the use of questions. This can be a strong manipulative weapon against women, because we have been taught not only that we must answer all questions asked of us, but we must also answer immediately and truthfully. Manipulators rely on that when they use questions dishonestly.

One example of a manipulative "trap" question is a "why" question. Although "why" questions can also be used appropriately, without hidden motives, more frequently "why" questions are not questions at all, but disguised statements or accusations. Putting a statement in a "why" question form evades responsibility for the statement. Typically the person asking already knows the answer, but is really trying to corner you or to start an argument. Other questions can be used in the same deceptive way:

Why Question	_Really Means_
"Why were you so late?"	"I don't think you should have been so late."
"Why can't you keep your room clean?"	"I don't think you should leave your room so messy."
"Why were you so rude with me?"	"I don't think you should be so rude with me."

Deceptive Questions	_Really Means_
(A parent, knowing the daughter/son has _not_ taken the garbage out yet):	
"Have you taken out the garbage?"	"I want you to take out the garbage."
(A spouse, knowing the other has _not_ called the restaurant to make dinner reservations):	
"Have you called the restaurant for reservations?"	"I want you to call the restaurant to make dinner reservations."

The peril in using questions manipulatively is that you teach others not to trust your questions. If asked a manipulative "why" question, an assertive woman may decide not to answer. She knows she doesn't _have_ to answer any question she's asked. An especially effective reply to the why question or deceptive question is, "Why do you ask?" This usually causes the questioner to say what she/he really means.

Another manipulative approach is the use of particular phrases that actually mean the opposite of what they sound. These, again, are designed to allow the manipulator to avoid taking responsibility. Some common examples of these "red flag" words and phrases are:

Red Flag Phrase	_Really Means_
"I don't know."	"I really do know but I don't want to take responsibility."
"I can't."	"I won't."

"I'll try."   "I won't."

"I should."   "I don't want to," or "I won't."

When you hear these phrases, mentally send up a little red flag to signal you to be prepared for a deceptive statement. Unless you really mean it, avoid using these phrases yourself.

Deactivate Your Buttons

A third manipulative tactic is "word loading." Only people who know you fairly well can use this one to manipulate you, because it depends on being able to identify your vulnerabilities, or "buttons." The manipulator will try to get to you by pushing your button. If you are sensitive about your weight, a manipulator can push your weight button by calling you a "fat slob" or "hefty." If you are sensitive about your intelligence, the manipulator can push your intelligence button by calling you "ignorant" or "brainy." If you hate to let anyone down, a manipulator can simply say, "you have disappointed me."

The best protection against this kind of manipulation is to identify what your buttons are. Then you can practice deactivating them by learning *not* to react automatically, so a would-be manipulator can't catch you off balance. With a friend, make up your button list. Exchange lists, and read each vulnerability aloud as realistically as possible, while you practice *not* responding to them. Use this check list to identify the buttons that apply to you and include some of your own.

BUTTON LIST
* Being told I disappoint someone.
* Being told I am unreliable or untrustworthy.
* Being told that I smoke too much, bite my nails, or some other bad habit.
* Being told that I am overweight (or underweight).
* Being teased about my freckles, new hair style, style of dress.
* Being ridiculed or teased about my sex, home town, accent, race, or income bracket.
* Other items that make you feel vulnerable:

Not responding will involve controlling your facial muscles so you don't reflexively smile or giggle when somebody pushes your button.

Practice relaxation as you listen to your friend. What you are doing is exercising your choice not to react, and giving yourself a feeling of control. When you can go through all of your buttons on your lists without reacting with undue anxiety or hostility, you will have made it difficult for the buttons to control you, and you can thwart a button-pusher's attempts to manipulate you. This isn't as easy as it sounds. If you are unable to deactivate your buttons alone, a professional counselor or therapist can provide you with the extra support you may need.

Counter-Manipulation

There are two major counter-manipulation techniques you can use when you feel you are being set up as a victim. By using counter-manipulation, you refuse to be manipulated and you promote assertive communication. The first technique is to respond to what is *said*, not to what you know is *meant*. In our first example with the two roommates, Allison could have responded only to what Isabel actually *said*, instead of responding to what she knew Isabel meant:

THE 2-FOR-1 ROOMMATE, TAKE 3

Allison: "Isabel, I'm sorry to have to bring this up, but Irv spends more time here than you do. I really wish he'd find his own place."

Isabel: "Gee, I thought you liked him — he sure likes you, you know. And he is looking for work but nobody appreciates his talent enough to hire him."

Allison: "I'm glad to hear he's looking. I know he'll want his own place so prospective employers can reach him."

Isabel: "Come on, Allison, he's a good guy. You're not going to get on your high horse and kick him out, are you?"

Allison: "He is a good person and I know you want to make sure he has every opportunity to succeed, including a place of his own."

In this example, Allison gets around the immediate impasse and avoids becoming a victim, but this strategy won't solve the problem in the long run — a forthright, assertive conversation is needed for that. This can be an effective defensive tactic, however.

READING BETWEEN THE LINES

A second strategy to short-circuit manipulation and encourage assertive communication is getting the manipulator to admit what she/he really wants. There are three parts to the process:

• *Parroting*: Repeating back exactly what was said to you.

- *Summarizing*: Verifying what was said by summarizing it and asking for acknowledgment.
- *Reflecting*: Reading between the lines, as in "you seem angry with me."

To see how these work, let's go back to our roommates again. This time, Allison gets Isabel to say what she really means:

Allison: "Isabel, Irv spends more time here than you do. It's time he found his own place."

Isabel: "Gee, I thought you liked him — he sure likes you, you know. And he is looking for work, but nobody appreciates his talent enough to hire him."

Allison: (parroting) "You didn't realize I liked Irv?"

Isabel: "He's so misunderstood. He tries, he really does. You're an educated woman, I would think you could understand that."

Allison: (summarizing) "You mean he's having a hard time right now, and you don't want to let him down?"

Isabel: "Of course. Anybody can see that, even you."

Allison: (reflecting) "You seem angry about it."

Isabel: "There you go again!"

Allison: (reflecting) "Isabel, you do seem upset to me."

Isabel: "Well, maybe a little. I'm only trying to help him out."

Allison: "I would be upset, too."

Isabel: "You would?"

Allison: "Sure. You are in a tough spot. Let's see if we can come up with a couple of ways to handle it that would work for both of us."

Isabel: "Well, okay. You could always move out, you know."

Allison: "Let's talk about other alternatives, shall we?"

This dialogue produced assertive — not perfect — communication. Both Allison and Isabel felt good about its progress. Allison faced up to her roommate problem, Isabel expressed herself honestly, and the issue, at last, is on the table.

When you try these strategies, keep in mind that it may take a while to accomplish your goals, but the results are worth the effort. Keep your voice even and well-modulated. It takes some self-control and patience, but if you do that, and learn to use the other counter-manipulation guidelines we've presented, you can be confident that you don't have to consent to being a helpless "victim" of even an experienced "set up operator's" plans to blackmail or manipulate you. You can be an assertive woman.

Summary

Manipulation is a matter of playing fast and loose with both circumstances and people until a desired goal is achieved: he feels so guilty that he won't play golf today and spend time with me instead; she's so uncomfortable and self-conscious after I asked her that question about her weight that she won't be able to upstage me for once. What is said produces anxiety, guilt, remorse, or some other uncomfortable reaction in another person, often resembling a jab at a particularly tender spot. And precisely because a manipulative exchange is indirect, a manipulator can always deny that she or he had any dishonorable or hidden intentions.

At the same time it's important to remember that manipulation is not always a conscious, deliberate, calculated strategy. The indirect approach, focused as it is on motivation through guilt or regret, is one way to get what you want if you don't have the courage or the skill to be straightforward. It may have been the only way you could get what you wanted as a child in your family, for example, if direct assertive approaches were thought rude or impolite.

In this chapter, we've defined manipulation and illustrated ways to recognize it and respond to it. We have also looked at some of the more persistent forms of manipulation that you may recognize in your own behavior. Manipulation is directly opposite assertiveness in one key way: accepting responsibility for one's own feelings and decisions is a hallmark of assertiveness, while manipulative, indirect encounters are focused on avoiding or denying responsibility.

Although manipulation can sometimes be effective in the short run, the price is *very* high: when the manipulator's intentions are discovered, the relationship is diminished (or even finished), and the "victim" thinks primarily of revenge.

Suggested Reading

Games Mother Never Taught You: Corporate Gamesmanship for Women by Betty L. Harragan. New York: Warner Books, 1989.

Chapter 15

Asserting Your Sensuality

To look at me, you'd never suspect I was a semi-nonorgasmic woman. This means it was possible for me to have an orgasm — but highly unlikely.

To me, the term "sexual freedom" meant freedom from having to have sex. And then along came Good Vibrations. And was I surprised! Now I am a regular Cat on a Hot Tin Roof.

"Trudy, the Bag Lady"
— Lily Tomlin and Jane Wagner
The Search for Signs of Intelligent Life in the Universe

In the mid-1970's, when *The Assertive Woman* was new, the United States in the throes of the sexual revolution. A flood of how-to books accompanied this sudden lifting of the veil of human sexuality. Some of this material was very helpful; some was destructive, inaccurate, and sexist. Psychologist and author Albert Ellis clearly described what's wrong with many of the most popular books on sex in his excellent book, *The Sensuous Person: Critique and Corrections*. Masters and Johnson's widely reported research on sexuality was also extremely helpful in dispelling sexual myths.

What progress have we made in matters sexual? After experiencing a sexual revolution, dropping old taboos and creating new ones, are we better off today? Have we regressed? And what does the 21st century hold for us?

A "Her"storical Perspective

In 1972, the Boston Women's Health Book Collective published their first edition of *Our Bodies, Ourselves*, a breakthrough compendium of women's health information. A general guide to women's physical health issues, the book exhorted women to take responsibility for their own well-being.

In 1975, Lonnie Barbach in her book, *For Yourself: The Fulfillment of Female Sexuality*, advanced the concept of personal liberation for women as sexual human beings. She suggested that women could ---- and should ---- assume full responsibility for their sexuality. Not only did Barbach say women deserved as many orgasms as they wanted, she gave explicit exercises to assist them in reaching maximum orgasmic potential.

Sexual liberation meant freedom to choose the kinds of sexual activities and stimulation that were most pleasurable. And it meant the freedom *not* to do what failed to meet your values or needs ---- freedom to be in control of the most intimate part of your life.

The 1980's produced a crescendo of exciting information about female sexuality. The "G-Spot," named after German gynecologist and sex researcher, Ernst Grafenberg, was rediscovered. His theory that there are two kinds of orgasms ---- clitoral and vaginal, including female ejaculation ---- resurrected an old controversy, and opposed Masters and Johnson's sex research.

Then Lonnie Barbach's second book, *For Each Other: Sharing Sexual Intimacy*, gave women a complete program for dealing with the complex physical and psychological aspects of sexual satisfaction in relationships. And yes, it did include a G-Spot stimulation exercise, along with many other exercises to promote sexual expression.

Meanwhile, women felt stepped-up social pressure to enhance their sexuality. "Satisfaction" was no longer enough: only virtuosa sexual performances would do.

By the mid-1980's the media declared the sexual revolution "over," and in the 1990s, the major focus was the AIDS epidemic, sexually transmitted diseases, abortion rights, and the sexual abuse of children.

Improved education and greater access to information has dramatically increased our awareness of these problems. We no longer feel free to experiment with multiple sexual partners; the dangers are too great. More than ever in the past two decades, we are forging successful monogamous relationships. New popular books reflect this trend. In *Love Skills*, for example, Linda De Villers describes how to maintain, deepen, and keep love alive over the long term by integrating sex, intimacy, and communication skills.

Some Positive Changes

Although we still wrestle with conflicting societal messages, new taboos, and increasingly complex challenges to our sensual and sexual freedoms, there is a strong emerging commitment in women and in men to achieve balance and mutuality in sexual relationships. Old traditions are crumbling. We are beginning to see positive changes.

In the 1996 edition of their assertiveness classic, *Your Perfect Right*, psychologists Robert Alberti and Michael Emmons describe past and current sexual expectations for women and men. Here are a few ideas adapted from their list:

* Women expect equality today, rather than passivity.
* Women initiate and communicate their enjoyment rather than remain silent.
* Women are becoming straightforward, honest and confident sexually.
* Men are becoming much more expressive emotionally —— they demonstrate a new openness.
* Macho male expectations are giving way to vulnerability, involvement, gentleness and patience.
* Equality and responsiveness in men is replacing exploitation and score keeping.

We cannot overstate the importance of mutuality; the sensually assertive woman shares much more sexual and sensual responsibility than did the docile doves of the past.

What is Sensuality?

Sensuality involves not only an appreciation of your bodily senses but also an ability to connect with your environment through sight, sound, smell, taste, and touch in a direct, straightforward way. The assertive woman feels alive, energetic, and awake to life.

Allison can go to an art show and experience it in a completely *visual* way that is unique and personal for her; she does not feel compelled to provide intellectual interpretations for those around her or to justify her likes and dislikes. She can fully enjoy something regardless of what others think. Similarly, music, the *sounds* outdoors, even her own voice, are all sources of pleasure.

You need not be shy about your sense of *taste*: explore different tastes, food, drink, or the tastes of your lover. Keep your body clean, and do not be afraid of how you may taste to your lover. Allison does not feel obligated to buy products designed to make her taste or smell unlike her own clean, beautiful, natural self. An assertive woman need not be paranoid about the way she tastes or smells.

Take full advantage of your sense of *touch*. Compare the softness of your own skin to the softness of a rose petal, or another woman's skin, or to the head of the penis. Allison is not inhibited about sensing her environment through touch. This extends, of course, into sexuality. Your sexuality can be expressed along with your sensual self, it is not limited to genital sex. It includes the pleasure derived from all your senses.

The Sensually Assertive Woman

The assertive woman becomes sensually assertive by getting to know herself better. She experiences herself and her environment freely and joyously through all of her senses — sight, taste, smell, sound, and touch. She explores her sexual attitudes to learn where she may be inhibited. She also explores her physical self through techniques that range from reading about female physiology to actually exploring her own body through masturbation, taking a look at another woman's body closely, or looking at herself with mirrors.

Believing that her own sensual and sexual needs and desires are legitimate — as real as any other feelings she has — is an important first step to becoming sensually assertive. The assertive woman knows that she has choices about how to express her sensuality. Nothing is wrong if she chooses for her own pleasure something that is not destructive to another person.

The sensually assertive woman explores her environment with others. She feels free to discuss sexuality with other women and with men. She strives for mutuality in a sexual relationship; she knows that she and her partner can exchange roles, that they can experiment with various levels of passivity or assertiveness in lovemaking.

Know Thyself. This step is very active and may involve an exploration of your own fantasy life. You can learn a great deal from your fantasies, and come to a greater acceptance of your sensual and sexual preferences. Self-knowledge can liberate you from a passive, solely responsive sex life.

Knowing your preferences also includes exploration of your body. It is important for *you* to know what feels good to you instead of passively expecting your partner to read your mind. You should not be afraid to explore your body's sensations and responses. The most personal and accurate way to learn about your own sexuality is through masturbation. This, of course, is a *choice* you have as a woman. We are not writing a defense of masturbation, but strongly suggest that you consider how masturbation may assist you in becoming a more sensually assertive woman. Perhaps you have not allowed yourself to consider the knowledge and research about masturbation which is available to you.

Express Yourself. Once you accept the legitimacy of your own sensuality, you need to be able to express it directly and honestly. You can do this with and without words. The important thing is that *you do it*. It's dishonest to pretend to be interested only in giving pleasure or in liking no more than what you get by chance!

New Expressions. Another aspect of becoming more sensually assertive is to allow yourself to open up to different kinds of sensual/sexual expression. This means looking at other possibilities besides the standard penis/vagina, man-on-top, male-initiated, orgasm-oriented sexuality. Being assertive means learning that you have choices and then feeling free to exercise these options.

In her 1991 book, *How to Make Love All the Time,* popular Los Angeles psychotherapist Barbara DeAngelis offers a quiz to find out if you're hoping your partner will read your mind when making love so you won't have to ask for what you really want or express how you feel. Her list of some of the common ways you may be relying on "ESP" when you make love may help you see that you have a communications problem, so you can start working to change it. Otherwise, the result will be built-up resentment, frustration and a decrease of passion in your relationship.

You'll enjoy finding out how much you rely on "ESP" when you make love, and want to do something about it. The solution, of course, is to communicate with your partner about what you like and don't like, what you're afraid of, and what makes lovemaking a "10" for you. At first you might find such honesty scary, but the result (we promise) will be a more passionate relationship.

A Sexual Look at Allison and Her Friends

In the chart on the next page, we've outlined some of the ways the "Four Women We All Know" might exercise their sexual options.

FOUR WOMEN WE ALL KNOW [HOW THEY MIGHT EXERCISE THEIR SEXUAL OPTIONS]

	Characteristics	Thoughts	Expressions	Feelings	Body Language	Her Options
DORRIE DOORMAT	Hesitant Shy	"He hurt my feelings by telling me I'm not sexy tonight."	"I'm sorry I'm not sexy."	Hurt Irritated	Hidden	"No way! I could *never* say anything."
AUGUSTA AGGRESSIVE	Demanding Pushy Insistent	"He's gotta change. He'd better learn some new techniques!"	"Can't you get with it? Everyone is into this."	Hostile	Confrontive	"If he can't measure up, I'll find someone who can."
ISABEL INDIRECT	Devious Manipulative Sneaky	"Ugh! Sex tonight... I'll fake a headache."	Takes some Tylenol, looks distressed, sighs and rubs her head.	Disgusted	Subversive	"Make excuses. Develop a 'condition.'"
ALLISON ASSERTIVE	Honest Open Straightforward	"There hasn't been enough foreplay for me to be ready for intercourse yet."	"I'd like us to take a little more time tonight. I'd enjoy more foreplay before intercourse."	Positive Bright	Open Forthright	Express herself. Tell him (in a caring way) what she likes.

"Dr. Truth's" Personal Sensuality Survey

These questions are intended as a first step toward becoming sensually assertive.

* Have you ever indulged a desire to look at a person or thing that you found beautiful or interesting?
* How do you feel about smelling your natural body odors and those of your lover?
* Have you ever explored anything other than food with your tongue and let yourself really taste it?
* Under what circumstances do you let yourself sing out loud?
* How do you feel about making sounds or talking during lovemaking?
* Are there taboo words that you don't dare utter aloud to your lover?
* Why do you make love?
* Do you feel guilty when you masturbate?
* When you have sexual intercourse, do you always expect to have an orgasm? If not, where does this leave you and how do you feel?
* Do you always expect the same level or orgasmic response?
* Have you ever experienced sexual or sensual attraction toward another woman?
* If you are already committed to one person, how do you handle your sexual attraction toward others?
* If there is no lover in your life now, do you feel worthless?
* Does your self-image depend more on what you think and feel about yourself or upon what you believe others feel and think about you?
* How do you communicate to your lover what you expect in your love-making?
* Do you have fantasies that you would like to act out?
* How do you share these fantasies with your lover?
* Who initiates experimentation in your lovemaking?

SENSUAL FANTASY

In your journal, write down, in as much detail as possible, your favorite sensual fantasy. Then consider sharing this fantasy with your sexual partner or someone to whom you feel close. Remember, sensuality includes more than sex.

EXCHANGING SEXUAL ROLES

This next exercise involves making a sincere effort to act out a role as honestly as you possibly can. Switch roles for five minutes with your sexual partner; "try on" each other's behavior. If one of you is more passive or assertive, be sure to emphasize that when you switch. Exchange names, clothes, or any other props that will best help you to enact the other person. You can try this on three different levels:

a) Focus on a domestic or routine situation you two usually get into around the house.

b) Give each other a massage, taking turns, and role-play how you see your partner giving the massage.

c) Switch roles in your love-making, including verbal as well as non-verbal actions. This one may take more than five minutes!

After you have tried this role-reversal, discuss how you felt about it, using the following questions as a guide:

* Were you surprised at what your partner did or said?
* How did you "read" certain things?
* What did you learn that was new?
* Were you able to laugh with each other?
* How can you best deal with each other's preferences?

Sexuality and Safety

In this day and age it doesn't pay to have a passive attitude about sex. Just as we have learned to manage time, communications, or a career, it is now in our best interest to learn about "sexual management."

Sexual abuse has become a major area of concern and study. It takes many forms, from obscene telephone calls to rape. In the past, most information about sexual assault focused on the most obvious — rape by a stranger. However, statistics show that acquaintance or "date rape" occurs where there is familiarity and trust — in a seemingly safe relationship. In *No is Not Enough: Helping Teenagers Avoid Sexual Assault*, authors Caren Adams, Jennifer Fay, and Jan Loreen-Martin presented a continuum of "force." Their framework makes clear that the difference between consenting sex and sexual assault is not the *sex*, but the degree of *force* used. There is no force in truly consensual sex between two partners. But force can be subtle or overt; it ranges from seduction to bribery or coercion, to acquaintance rape, to maximum-force stranger rape. Avoiding sexual assault is not merely staying away from dark alleys.

It is also the ability to read and respond to more subtle, and dangerous, sexual signals ---- without hesitation or apology.

Women are now learning to be even more cautious, especially in bars. Men may slip the "date rape" drug, "Rohypnol," into their drinks, which renders them nearly unconscious, and makes them prime rape candidates.

Harassment. Authors Adams, Fay and Loreen-Martin define sexual harassment as "any repeated and unwanted sexual attention (verbal or physical) ranging from advances, suggestive looks, jokes, innuendoes to explicit propositions and assaults which cause discomfort to a woman and interfere with her job or school performance." Men can be harassed too, but women are harassed many times as often and suffer more serious results: an inability to concentrate, anger, diminished self-confidence, sharply reduced job effectiveness. (See sidebar on Harassment, pages 200-201.)

Anita Hill's 1991 charge that Clarence Thomas had sexually harassed her when they worked together started a national dialog on the subject. Five years later, when Senator Robert Packwood of Oregon was accused of sexual harassment, he was forced to resign his Senate seat.

Whose Fault Is It, Anyway? Taking responsibility for oneself is a quality of maturity. However, taking responsibility for what other people say or do is a trap. Too often women believe that if they "had only tried harder" they could have avoided becoming targets for sexual abuse. Courts and other institutions have often fostered blame-the-victim thinking, colluding with men in rape cases by inferring that if the woman hadn't looked so sexy or in some other way led the rapist on, he wouldn't have reached the point of no return. How unfair it has been to blame women for inciting "uncontrollable passions" in men! Rape is an issue of power, not sexuality. Women must be aware that their powerlessness is much more an incentive to male attackers than is their sexuality.

How Does An Assertive Woman Avoid Abuse? A confident, assertive approach is one of the most effective defenses against sexual assault. Silence, pleas, or tears all demonstrate to a would-be attacker that a woman is, indeed, helpless.

An assertive attitude will also help you to ask a sexual partner for proof that he or she is free from AIDS, and to insist that a condom is always used. Because they invite respect, healthy self-esteem and an assertive approach may be your greatest source of safety.

Future Forecasts

As we have pointed out in this chapter, "the sexual revolution" was only a beginning step in advancing the full expression of human sexuality. Researchers uncovered new data that dispelled old myths. Yet, as traditional obstacles crumbled, there were new hurdles to overcome.

One of the many paradoxes still unresolved is that we don't really know how to use all this freedom and sexual information. Just because the media have kept information flowing about G- Spots, AIDS, abortion, impotence, orgasms, condoms and pornography doesn't mean that everyone understands or is even willing to read or listen.

There is still a sexual cover-up in our society: sexual issues are not addressed directly in public. We can meet the challenge *individually* in the 21st century, however. Let's break open the communication barriers. Hone your skills at negotiating with your romantic partner for safe sex. Free yourself to discuss personal issues about everything from body odors, AIDS, and contraception to sexual preferences.

For you, asserting your sensuality may mean tuning in to the "Dr. Ruth" show and discussing your reactions. It may be reading this chapter with your partner and completing the exercises together. Other books on sexuality listed below will enhance your sensual assertiveness as well.

Suggested Reading

Confidence: Finding It and Living It, by Barbara DeAngelis, Ph.D. Carson, California: Hay House, 1995.

Dr. Ruth's Guide to Good Sex, by Dr. Ruth Westheimer. New York: Warner Books, 1986.

How to Make Love All the Time, by Barbara DeAngelis., Ph.D. New York: Dell Publishing, 1991.

Love Skills: More Fun than You've Ever Had with Sex, Intimacy and Communication, by Linda De Villers, Ph.D. San Luis Obispo, California: Impact Publishers, Inc., 1996.

The New Our Bodies, Ourselves, by the Boston Women's Health Book Collective. New York: Simon & Schuster, 1992.

The Search for Signs of Intelligent Life in the Universe by Jane Wagner. New York: Harper and Row Publishers, 1991.

Your Perfect Right: A Guide to Assertive Living (Seventh Edition), by Robert E. Alberti, Ph.D., and Michael L. Emmons, Ph.D. San Luis Obispo, California: Impact Publishers, 1995.

Chapter 16

The Anger In You

i wasn't doing nothing
just driving about
screaming at the dark
letting it out
that's all i was doing
just
letting it out...

...i'm just a creature
who is looking
for a little release
i said
and what's so wrong with screaming...
—— Dory Previn, "Twenty-mile Zone"*

Dory Previn's lyrics poignantly illustrate the taboo that women have endured against overt expression of anger. Women have been taught that it is not lady-like or feminine to show that they are angry. We have been intimidated by the threat of being called "bitchy," "castrating," "nagging," "aggressive," or "masculine." The Compassion Trap further prevents women from expressing anger by making us feel guilty for even thinking of expressing it. Women smile sweetly and grit their teeth, hoping that no hint of their anger or hostility will be exposed. After all, "someone has to keep peace in the family." Guess who that someone is?

Because anger is such a powerful emotion, it is difficult for many women —— who already labor under a sense of powerlessness —— to express, or even to acknowledge. It's frightening for them to "play around with anger," since they view it almost as a deadly weapon that leads to violence.

---

*Published by Mediarts Music, Inc./Bouquet Music.©
Used by permission of the author.

Actually, the constructive ways to handle anger that we'll talk about in this chapter can help *prevent* violence. Research shows that much domestic violence, even homicide, is caused by people who could not deal with their anger in honest, non-destructive ways.

We can learn about anger, accept it, and learn to express it assertively. We need no longer deny that very real ---- and very normal ---- part of ourselves.

"Do I Have to Express My Anger?"

Not necessarily.

Before we get serious about ways to *express* your anger effectively, let's consider briefly some other ways to handle it. There are many ---- more than you might think ---- but to simplify our discussion, they fall into three broad categories: *awareness, prevention,* and *denial.* The first two are healthy, and part of the solution. Denial, of course, is part of the problem.

Awareness means getting in touch with what triggers anger in you. Knowing yourself ---- your feelings, attitudes and beliefs about how things "ought to be" ---- is the key to recognizing anger when (and even before) it occurs. When you know what you expect, you can anticipate disappointment and figure out just what makes you angry. You're on your way to handling it better.

Prevention means learning to stop anger before it starts. Not every situation is worthy of your anger, and it's important to sort out your priorities so you don't sweat the small stuff. Among the preventive strategies you may want to explore: learning to relax, giving up unrealistic expectations, changing irrational beliefs.

Denial of anger is a tactic some women employ to cover up their angry feelings. They deny that their anger exists, choosing instead to say, "Oh, that's okay. I'm fine. No problem." Such "stuffed" anger, unexpressed but not forgotten, can lead to any number of physical and/or psychological ailments: headaches, arthritis, gastrointestinal disturbances, skin problems, and more. Awareness and prevention are important tools for dealing with the anger in your life, and we encourage you to develop them fully by studying one of the excellent books we've listed at the end of this chapter, or by attending an anger workshop or seeing a therapist who specializes in anger work. (Caution: Don't be satisfied with pillow pounding and shouting exercises which purportedly "release" anger. These techniques may help get you started, but research shows that the only lasting procedure for dealing with anger is to work out some *resolution* within yourself or with the person or problem that triggered the anger in the first place.)

Because this book is concerned primarily with *expressing* yourself assertively, that will be the focus of our discussion and the exercises in the following pages. Keep in mind, however, that you still have a choice. Sometimes the assertive thing to do is walk away.

First Steps in Handling Anger

Recognizing your anger is the first step toward learning how to deal with it. Once you notice the feeling, acknowledge it as real. Women deny their anger even after they recognize it because they don't believe they have a valid reason for it. They may feel it is aggressive, or unreasonable. Recognizing anger is not just an intellectual exercise; it is actually the only way to be in touch with the emotional feeling that is anger. Your anger is real, and it belongs to you.

Once you accept your angry feelings, *identify the source* of your anger. Where is it coming from? It is easy to blame somebody else for your anger either out of guilt or perhaps to save face in an embarrassing situation. It may be more acceptable to get angry over something small and irritating rather than face the real cause of your anger, say, a big disappointment or unfulfilled expectation.

Many women have lived with buried anger for years. It seems a woman in this position must, when first she becomes aware of her anger, go through an "angry phase," in which she is angry a great deal of the time. This phase may last a few months, until she learns to deal with her anger *appropriately* and *realistically*. It is in this last step that assertiveness is such a powerful tool.

Anger Is Not Aggression!

Anger is an emotion ---- a feeling ---- a mental and physical reaction to a violation of your person, territory, attitudes or beliefs. Most of us get angry if we feel used, or put down, or stepped on. Let's debunk one popular myth about anger: *anger is not aggression*. Anger is a legitimate *feeling;* everybody gets angry at times. As you know from earlier chapters of this book, aggression is a style of *behavior* ---- a pushy way to *express* anger. There are a variety of ways to express anger, including Dorrie's denial, Isabel's indirect expression, Augusta's aggression (including hostility and violence), and Allison's assertion. The exercises and examples in the rest of this chapter will help to clarify these definitions.

Denial of Anger

We hear a lot about "denial" these days. We're using it here as a name for "stuffing" your annoyance or irritation, not really admitting that you are feeling angry: "I'm fed up with this job. No, I'm not angry. I'm just sick and tired. That's all."

This way of handling anger is most often Dorrie's style; she mistakenly thinks that she is being assertive by complaining. Unfortunately, however, she usually complains to the wrong source, as the following situation shows.

"MIRROR, MIRROR ON THE WALL . . ."

Dorrie: "I bought this face cream to tighten my pores and clear up my complexion. Instead my face is covered with a rash, and now I look awful. This cream is useless and a total waste of money."

Allison: "You sound pretty mad about it. Why don't you return it and get your money back?"

Dorrie: "Oh, why bother? I'm not really angry. I'm just disgusted with my skin problems. I should try something else."

Indirect Anger Expression

Another form of anger expression is "indirect." This is Isabel's forte. She directs her angry feelings into attempts to make the other person feel guilty. Here is an example of Isabel being angry with her friend in an indirect way.

"LEAVE ME"

John: "I'm leaving now, and won't be able to see you again until next week."

Isabel: "Of course, I don't mind. Go right ahead. It doesn't bother me. I've been lonely before. I'm just disappointed that you want to leave me at a time like this. But, go right ahead anyway."

It is important to mention that women also express anger indirectly through their sexuality. Sometimes "holding out" sexually seems the only way a woman who feels powerless communicates her resentment. If you find yourself holding back, ask yourself why you're feeling distant. Is it because you're angry? What about? Are you frustrated because you did not handle another situation assertively? Also, if you find yourself being overly sweet in a situation, look inside yourself to see if you are compensating for some residue of anger that you have not confronted.

Sometimes when Isabel is overly sweet (or even condescending and patronizing), she is expressing hostility indirectly. Of course, the other person may respond with indirect anger!

"SOME OF MY BEST FRIENDS ARE BLACK"
Isabel: "Just because you're black doesn't matter to me. I don't even notice your hair and all that stuff. I really like you. You're just like anybody else. It doesn't bother me the way you talk ---- what do you call it now? Ebonics? I'm glad you joined our group."

Angela: "Thanks, Isabel, I'm really glad you let me into your group. I'll try not to notice that the rest of you are white. Of course, we think you're racist because you're always dissing us. That doesn't make me angry, but I do feel weird and left out sometimes."

Isabel may not recognize that Angela is repaying her insults. Isabel will not change her behavior until she is directly confronted with her put-downs and their effect.

Aggressive Anger Expression
Although aggression may be an overt, direct expression of anger, it usually is an overreaction. For example, Augusta often feels that she can only express her anger with insults, even physical abuse. You need not use aggression to convince people that you mean business. Being assertive is enough to get this point across. However, when people have been frustrated in their attempt to express anger assertively, they may see aggression (even violence) as the only option left.

Let's look at a situation which ignites so much anger that it can easily result in violent behavior.

CRY RAPE
Augusta's friend Joyce has been raped. She asks Augusta to help her go to the police. When Joyce and Augusta arrive, they are both treated disrespectfully. A police officer asks Joyce what she did to seduce the guy into going after her. Then he insinuates that she probably enjoyed it, or that she may be lying just to get some poor guy into trouble. Of course, this makes both women furious. Augusta calls the officer a "sexist jerk." She threatens the officer, saying that he probably rapes women whenever

he has the chance, that women have no rights when it comes to law enforcement, that all men are pigs and back each other up in doing violence to women. She is ready to spit on him, when he grabs her arm and shakes her. They get into a tussle and Augusta is arrested for assaulting a police officer.

Augusta's anger is controlling her. She has a legitimate reason to be angered by the officer's humiliating remarks and behavior, but her behavior only escalates the tension and provides no support for Joyce.

Assertive Anger Expression

It's easy to recognize assertive anger because it is expressed clearly and directly. It is not physically or verbally abusive. Allison, in Augusta's situation, would let the officer know that she is angry by stating her feelings this way:

Allison: "I'm here with my friend because she has been raped. This is not a joke. I am angry when you refuse to take her seriously. She has been humiliated once, and there is no need for her to be humiliated again. I would appreciate it if you treated her with kindness and respect."

Action Exercises

We started out this chapter with Dory Previn screaming on the roadway. Now we are going to ask you to do some "screaming" too, and some other exercises that will help you develop better skills for dealing with anger. Find a comfortable private place, get together with a partner and try the following exercises.

X-Y-Z-1-2-3

Sit facing another person. One of you choose "letters" and the other "numbers" to shout randomly at each other. Before you start, think of a situation or person with whom you are angry and get in touch with those feelings. When you are ready, begin shouting simultaneously for at least two minutes. Be aware of whether or not you begin with a bang and soon fade; note if you are sidetracked by what the other person is shouting. This happens regularly with women: if they started with letters they suddenly find themselves shouting their partner's numbers. Practice until you feel that you can stick with your own anger consistently. (Another valuable part of this exercise is to get used to how to make angry sounds and to take the sting out of hearing these sounds from others.)

THE "SILENT MOVIE" TECHNIQUE

Next, allow your body to express anger nonverbally. (This technique was developed by the late behavioral psychiatrist Michael Serber.) Face your partner and pretend that you are both in silent movies and that you are trying to communicate to one another how angry you are. Use facial expressions, gestures, and your body to convey angry feelings *without* talking.

GETTING INTO THE "TALKIES"

Now that you have practiced the verbal and nonverbal parts of anger, put them together in this next exercise: Repeat these phrases, using good eye contact, appropriate body language, and varied voice volume and tone:

"I feel angry right now."

"I don't like it when you ignore me."

"I am very upset about what you said/did."

"Stop that!"

"Pay attention to me when I'm talking to you!"

"I get *very* mad when I think I've been cheated."

Make up other phrases of your own. Give each other honest feedback on how well you communicated.

DISARMING AN ANGRY PERSON

When someone is very angry and is screaming and yelling at you, try the following exercise to disarm the anger. First, acknowledge with an assertive message that you definitely hear her/him. You can say, "I hear you," or perhaps, "I know you're angry at me." Often this acknowledgment will calm the person enough to enable you both to discuss the issue. If not, in a calm, assertive manner say something such as, "I really want to talk to you, but I cannot talk to you when you're screaming. As soon as you're calm, I will be happy to talk to you." You can repeat this until the person calms down. Then *listen*. However, if the screaming continues, you have the right to leave the situation. You can say that you are leaving until you both can hear each other out. Or, you can just leave! Women are notorious for hanging in there in an argument and often feel compelled to hold out until the bitter end. This is masochistic and totally unnecessary.

Before you try to disarm an angry person in a real life situation, practice this process with a friend until you feel sure about what you are doing.

You Can Choose Not to Express Yourself

Even when you express anger assertively, the person with whom you are angry may respond with backbiting, aggression, temper tantrums, over-apologizing or revenge. The assertive woman may choose *not* to assert herself when she is dealing with overly sensitive individuals, or if speaking up would be redundant. If you can see that another person is having difficulty, you may decide not to assert yourself at that moment ─── but the assertive woman knows the difference between appropriate understanding and the Compassion Trap. Remember too, that not all situations are worthy of your energy; sometimes it's an assertive choice just to let it go. Your emotional equilibrium is worth a lot!

Take Charge of Your Anger!

If you can see from our brief exploration of anger in this chapter that this is especially difficult for you, we encourage you to read more about the subject in one of the resources listed below. Consider carefully your responses to anger ─── your own and that of others ─── and seek the help of a qualified professional therapist if you find yourself:

....totally unable to express anger

....unaware of any feelings you'd call "angry."

....bursting into tears whenever you feel angry

....reacting aggressively or violently to minor annoyances

....often depressed about your life and relationships

....experiencing frequent violent or destructive thoughts about
      others or yourself.

Summary

A sensitive, complete approach to learning to deal with anger should include:

• *becoming aware of your angry feelings* (including steps for strongly and emotionally venting angry feelings in non-destructive ways ─── this is where pillow-pounding may fit.

• *developing greater tolerance* for situations which have sparked anger.

• *changing attitudes* which lead you to believe that life should be fair, non-hurtful.

• *learning to relax* in spite of minor annoyances.

• *learning and practicing new, assertive methods* to express your anger.

Your anger is a healthy and natural part of you. Listen to it, treat it with respect, express it assertively when it's appropriate ~~~ but don't let it control your life!

Suggested Reading

Anger: The Misunderstood Emotion, by Carol Tavris, Ph.D. New York: Simon & Schuster, 1982.

Anger Kills, by Redford Williams, M.D. and Virginia Williams, Ph.D. New York: HarperCollins, 1994.

Your Perfect Right: A Guide to Assertive Living (seventh edition), by Robert E. Alberti, Ph.D., and Michael L. Emmons, Ph.D. San Luis Obispo, California: Impact Publishers, 1995.

Chapter 17

Humor ---- We Need More of It!

*From birth to age 18, a girl needs good parents, from 18 to 35
she needs good looks, from 35 to 55 she needs a good personality,
and from 55 on she needs cash.*

---- Sophie Tucker

Cartoonist Nicole Hollander, in one of her "Sylvia" strips, shows Sylvia watching the infamous Enjoli perfume commercial: "I can bring home the bacon, fry it up in a pan... and never let you forget you're a man...." In the next panel, Sylvia speaks for real women everywhere when she concludes, "That woman must be on drugs."

Humor can be used to express love, affection, and caring, and to spotlight your quick wit. It can also be devastating when used as a weapon to wound others where it hurts most. Women have experienced humor largely as victims, as targets for countless bad jokes: "Did you hear the one about the mother-in-law...?" We laughed because we were expected to laugh.

As for expressing our own humor, it simply was not part of being a woman. Like anger, humor was not displayed freely by any woman who would remain a "lady": passive, reserved, demure, and quiet, seen but not heard, and certainly not laughing!

Women find it hard to trust humor, including their own, because it has so frequently been used against them. There's the woman who's elected treasurer for an organization, who jokes that she'd be pleased to take the job as long as the books don't have to balance to the penny; there's the woman librarian who misplaces dictionaries. We've learned to laugh, yes, but not at what was not really very funny to us. We've grinned and borne it.

While the tide has turned against many comic portrayals, women are still ridiculed for classic feminine traits, as well as for new liberated attitudes. Jokes about ethnic groups or the handicapped or the poor or the downtrodden are strenuously avoided, but women are fair game for cartoonists and comics, television writers and comedians and businessmen who want a snappy opening for a speech.

We have all heard old jokes like these, which are supposedly funny:

* "Who was that lady I saw you with last night?" "That was no lady, that was my wife!"

* Happiness is... discovering at the kindergarten pageant that when your son said his teacher was forty-two, he didn't mean her age.

* "You gave your mother-in-law a plant for her birthday?" "Yeah, poison ivy."

* "Look at that fender; were you in a wreck, Joe?" "No, this is my wife's car. You should see our garage door!"

* "Honey, we never seem to have any more conversations together." "O.K., so lie down and I'll talk to you."

In her book, *They Used to Call Me Snow White...but I Drifted,* Regina Barreca describes a woman executive who is new to a company and has just sat down to lunch in the official "old boys" lunchroom. As the only woman, she is eager to be accepted and liked. Suddenly, one of the top executives tells an "off-color joke" ― a joke with an obviously sexual innuendo. The men all laughed, but the woman wasn't sure how to respond. She felt the joke was offensive, but she remained quiet until the joke teller turned to her and apologized for "telling a dirty joke in front of a lady." The group waited to hear her response.

Although she had been uncertain until that moment about how she should handle the situation, it suddenly became very clear. She looked at him in the eye and smiled broadly. "In fact, you did not tell a dirty joke in front of a lady," she replied in her most kindly professional tone.

"You just told a dirty joke *to* a lady. Big difference." The rest of the group now laughed with the woman and at their respected colleague, and the tension in the room decreased noticeably.

As women begin to express themselves openly and assertively, they no longer want to laugh at unfunny jokes. They have the freedom to hone and use their own sense of humor, and to refuse to be passive victims of its misuse.

Sarcastic Humor

Using humor assertively takes practice. For starters, there is a big difference between its use and abuse. Sarcasm, a form of humor, is a powerful tool that can be particularly hostile, and is best left in the hands of comediennes like Roseanne, Joan Rivers or Ellen DeGeneres. If you have been the receiving end of sarcasm, you probably sensed anger and hostility passing for "humor."

Sarcasm and caustic wit are Isabel Indirect's favorite ways to be "funny." She is, of course, actually hostile and tries to upset you with her remarks. Isabel may say to a neighbor who was late for a morning meeting: "Late again, Ethel? You better cut out all that late-night drinking!" --- or to an overweight friend who is struggling with a diet --- "Sure, Mary, have some cake --- you are looking a little underweight today." Obviously, Isabel uses "humor" as a vehicle for insults and hostilities. Don't use sarcasm and "humorous insults" to express anger. It is better communicated assertively, directly and honestly.

The "Achilles Heel" humorist attacks others where it hurts most. Consider how Allison handles the Achilles Heel humorist in the following situations:

"YOU'RE NOT ONE OF THOSE WOMEN...?"

Achilles: "Allison, when are you going to do something with your life instead of just being a housewife?"

Allison: "You obviously have never met a Domestic Goddess before!"

Achilles: "Hey, Allison! Let's see what you're reading. Oh, no! You're not one of *those* women that reads silly romance novels!"

Allison: "Did you know that *those* women have more satisfying sex lives than non-readers? There's research to prove it!"

This style of humor is directed at a personal characteristic, habit, favorite pastime, or lifestyle of the victim. To the victim, of course, it is not funny at all. Allison responds to an Achilles Heel attack effectively with a quick retort, or simply by telling the attacker to stop. If you don't feel as confident with your comebacks as you do with telling the attacker to stop, give it a little practice. You don't have to make a witty remark at all if you don't want to. Directly expressing your annoyance is equally effective to stop an Achilles Heel attacker. The important thing to remember is to *act*, and not to be the quiet, passive victim.

Teasing

Teasing is another form of humor which involves "poking fun" at someone. Sometimes the use of subtle affectionate teasing can help overcome anxiety. Usually, however, teasing serves to alienate, and, taken to its extreme, teasing can be a kind of attack. At this point, teasing is an expression of aggression, not affection. Consider the following situation, for example:

"VIOLETS ARE RED, ROSES ARE BLUE . . ."

Allison is enrolled in a poetry class. Augusta Aggressive has persuaded Allison to let her read some of her poems. Augusta thinks that Allison's poems are the funniest things she's ever read, and asks Allison if she has considered doing comedy writing. Another friend, Isabel, joins in. Augusta reads some poems aloud and asks if Allison's poems aren't absolutely hysterical. Isabel joins Augusta in laughing at Allison's work. Allison had been spending a good deal of time with her poetry, and she is hurt and angered by Augusta's "teasing." Augusta and Isabel have alienated Allison with their "humor."

Allison has the option to put up with the teasing or to demand that it stop: "Come on, cut it out. I don't like to be teased about that."

If Allison chooses to assert herself and ask that the teasing stop, she will likely be teased some more: "What's wrong with you, can't you take a joke?" She can respond with the same request again, using the "broken record" technique.

We suggest that you review your use of teasing. Is it affectionate or aggressive and alienating? How have you felt when you've been teased to the point that it's not funny anymore? Try to be aware of how you use teasing, and beware of launching aggressive attacks. Tease sparingly and affectionately.

Humor — A Weapon Against Yourself

Women still use humor against themselves. Dorrie Doormat says, "I forgot my checkbook — isn't that just like a woman?" or "You know how I am — I'm just *lost* without my husband (ha ha)." In the guise of self-deprecating humor, Dorrie makes herself the bulls-eye for slings and arrows that are decidedly unfunny.

We are not suggesting that being an assertive woman means that you are humorless, or that you can't laugh at yourself. But you can use humor assertively by declining to use it as a weapon against yourself or others. Happily, humor enhances self-expression.

Giving yourself permission to *respond* to humorous situations, to laugh when you want to laugh, is the other component of assertive humor. How do you respond to situations you find funny?

Dorrie waits to see how others respond. If they laugh, she will, but she is careful to stop first, so she isn't "caught" laughing too much. She may also feel guilty because she is clearly enjoying herself.

Augusta, by contrast, laughs uproariously with little provocation. She laughs loud and long; it lets her steal the show and call attention to herself, but other people find her laughter overpowering.

Isabel, like Dorrie, may laugh to hide nervousness or insecurity, but often her laughter is thinly disguised hostility.

Allison laughs when she finds humor in a particular situation. She won't use her laughter to dominate others, and she doesn't feel guilty or anxious about laughing at something that is funny to her. She is aware of others' feelings and rights, and she will not "laugh in someone's face."

Healing Humor

"Laughter is the best medicine," as they say at *Reader's Digest*. Humor can be healing. It eases tensions when no other strategies work. It can melt an impossible conflict, bypass an impasse, soothe hurt feelings, and promote a sense of well-being.

Rosie O'Donnell has certainly proven that talk shows can be fun and healing. When her daytime television program debuted in 1996, network executives were astounded at her high ratings. They discovered that viewers had been turned off by standard-issue sleazy talk shows and jumped for a gentle, humorous program. The show's success soon forced rival programs to change their formats.

Lily Tomlin is another of our favorite healing humorists. She has blended laughter with compassion ever since her earliest TV days with the "Laugh-In" series. Tomlin's brand of humor reached thousands of people through her one-woman show "The Search for Signs of Intelligent Life in the Universe," which first opened on Broadway in 1984 and is now a standard in repertory theaters across the country. The script, written by her longtime collaborator, Jane Wagner, focuses on the female perspective of the latter part of the 20th century. The commentary is narrated by Tomlin as "Trudy," an outrageous bag lady who communicates with curious space aliens and who uses "awe- robics" every day. Tomlin's interpretation of Wagner's clever monologues brings out the funny side of the struggles and dilemmas experienced by contemporary women. Here are some examples:

On knowing what you want and being assertive ----
"Yes, I am having an affair. But not for long, I think. It's one thing to tolerate a boring marriage, but a boring affair does *not* make sense."

On rejecting a date at his place ----
"He invited me to his place. I told him I'd love to another time, but that I had my shift on the Rape Crisis Hot Line."

On being a pregnant woman in management ----
"No, I haven't told the office, it might affect my job. This morning I threw up at a board meeting. I was sure the cat was out of the bag, but no one seemed to think anything about it; apparently it's quite common for people to throw up at board meetings."

On the androgynous male ----
"I worry sometimes, maybe Bob has gotten too much in touch with his feminine side. Last night, I'm pretty sure, he faked an orgasm."

Scott Adam's wildly popular comic strip "Dilbert" has helped us to understand ---- and laugh at ---- America's corporate culture. In his 1996 book, *The Dilbert Principle*, Adams argues that swearing is the key to success for women in business. He claims that men are expected to swear, so there is no shock value when they do. But he says that it's very different for women; swearing can be shocking and attention-grabbing, and is a sign of female power.

Consider his scenario:
"A man comes to a woman's office and offers to show her a report. The woman responds by saying, 'Ah, shove it up your ass and die.' The man will be momentarily stunned. It is unlikely that he will pull up a chair.

Nor will he experience any bonding. He will probably back slowly out the door. The woman's productivity will skyrocket.

But what about the repercussions? The woman might someday need a favor from the man she has just verbally abused. Fortunately for her, all men are trained at birth to accept verbal abuse and get over it rather quickly.

And in the unlikely event that the man shows some hesitation to be helpful in the future, the situation can be smoothed over with the simple communication technique of saying, 'Do it now or I'll rip off your nuts and shove them down your throat.' "

Cathy Guisewite, another of the healing humorists, has been showing us how to laugh at ourselves through her popular "Cathy" cartoon character. In Guisewite's book, *Another Saturday Night of Wild and Reckless Abandon*, Cathy spends a good deal of time in restaurants. In one sequence, dining alone and noticing an attractive man across the room, Cathy summons the waitress ---- and her courage. She requests that "a dish of macaroni salad" be delivered to the man's table with her compliments. When the waitress hesitates, she exclaims, "Why are you looking at me like that? Haven't you ever seen an assertive woman in action before?" In the last panel, the waitress points Cathy out to the man; Cathy, meanwhile, has pulled the tablecloth over her head.

In another strip, Cathy and her friend Andrea are shown leaving a restaurant when Cathy decides to go back and complain about the food. Noting to Andrea that "women have to learn to stand up for themselves," she announces "You are about to witness the assertive woman in a restaurant!!" A defeated Cathy returns, in the final frame, telling Andrea, "The waitress demanded a bigger tip."

LAUGHING AT MYSELF — A TRUE STORY
By Stanlee

A funny thing happened today. I've been a little uptight lately — writing, not getting enough sleep, taking it all too seriously! I went out for a short errand to photocopy some material for this chapter on Humor (no joke!). I was in a hurry and feeling that I didn't have enough time.

When I arrived back home, I found the flight of stairs and banister leading up to my front door covered with what looked like 200 donuts! Yes, they were assorted and the aroma was maddening. Flowers and other little surprises had been artfully arranged amidst the donuts as well.

As my eyes scanned the stairs, focusing on all the sprinkles, sugar, drippy frosting and crumbs that would need to be cleaned up, I was furious. In thinking about the mess, I was so frustrated I actually considered sitting down and eating as many as I could!

While I was carting it all to the trash, sweeping and hosing away the remains, I recognized how upset I had become. My neighbors all came out to watch and thought it was terribly funny.

I asked myself what went wrong. Why didn't I think it was funny?

It had taken my friend a lot more time to put everything together than it took me to disassemble. I was tired but I was smiling.

The whole thing seemed so silly... me cleaning up all those donuts as if my life depended on it.

I laughed out loud at myself and wanted to share this story with you.

Express Your Humor

To express your sense of humor assertively, first embrace the idea that it's okay to express it.

Dorrie Doormat would not risk telling anyone else about something she thought was funny. She fears rejection and needs approval: "What if they don't think it's funny?" She may also feel anxious and guilty about finding humor in a serious situation, and would not joke about it.

Isabel Indirect uses humor as a vehicle for insults and hostilities. She often is an Achilles Heel humorist, hiding behind humor to attack others. Sometimes she uses humor to put herself down, or to bait the Compassion Trap for others.

Augusta Aggressive, on the other hand, is a regular comedian — she overuses humor. Others believe that to Augusta everything is a joke, and their own interests will not be considered seriously.

Allison Assertive knows that it's okay to express her sense of humor. She can say something funny without feeling unduly anxious or guilty, and without fear of rejection. Allison knows that some people will laugh and others won't, but exercising her right to say something she thinks is funny without harming others is most important to her.

Actively expressing your sense of humor means saying whatever is funny to *you*, as long as you aren't hard on yourself or someone else.

Humor Yourself

The first tender years of the Women's Movement were singularly devoid of any humor: the issues were deadly serious. As the years went by, jokes sprouted here and there, most of the best conceived by women themselves (Question: How many feminists does it take to change a light bulb? Answer: Five. One to change the bulb and four to form a support group). The difference, of course, was that now women were kidding themselves. We had enough perspective to find the humor in our achievements and our pitfalls.

Like any other skill, humor can be cultivated. Consider trying the following to strengthen your own humor power:

• Collect funny cartoons and jokes in a "Funny File." Refer to it frequently.

• Post funny stories, anecdotes, pictures, even fortunes from Chinese cookies on a bulletin board so you can get a chuckle every time you look at it. This has worked well for both authors. For example, Nancy's last three fortune cookies advised: 1) "For better luck, you have to wait until fall." 2) "For better luck, you have to wait until winter." 3) "For better luck, you have to wait until spring." No kidding.

• Don't be afraid to inject a little levity into business presentations. You don't want to be outrageous, but you can lighten your style enough to keep your audience attentive.

• Think of your own experiences, and try recasting them as short anecdotes or amusing stories. You might be surprised to discover that what was mortifying at the time is very funny later. A friend learned this when her intelligent young son, then eight, got bored and wanted to leave school one day at about noon, instead of the usual 2:30. He quickly wrote the following note to his teacher: "Please excuse Jeremy at noon today. He has to leave the state." He signed it, "Jeremy's Mother," in his eight-year-old's idea of her handwriting. Jeremy's mother received a call from the teacher, and after a few minutes, they were both laughing about it!

• Come up with your own "code words" that you can use when you feel under pressure and need to step back from a situation. Repeat them whenever you feel a downward, anxiety-driven spiral beginning, or to relieve tension.

• Build a video library of your favorite funny films. Do the same with books.

• Smile. It sounds trite, but research has shown that if you smile when you don't really feel like it, your emotions get the message and start to adapt to what's on your face! Conversely, if you frown, you actually spark the emotions commonly associated with frowning: worry, depression, frustration.

• Pick a funny role model and watch how she or he handles problems or crises. What would Julia Louis-Dreyfus (on TV's "Seinfeld") do? How about Candace Bergen? Lily Tomlin? Goldie Hawn? Bette Midler?

• Every day, find something funny in your own behavior, in a situation, or in another person's behavior. Describe what tickles your funny bone about this. Share your perception with someone else without *trying* to be a comedian. Instead focus on expressing the humor in such a way that you are inviting the other person to delight in your perception and laugh with you. Laughter is contagious. It's also healing, helpful and playful.

To respond assertively to something that you find humorous is to laugh, or smile, or chuckle about it. The important thing to remember is to express your humor, honestly and spontaneously, without feeling guilty or anxious about it, and without aggressively "taking over" every humorous situation. Your sense of humor is part of who you are; expressing it is part of being an assertive woman.

Smile!

Suggested Reading

Another Saturday Night of Wild and Reckless Abandon, by Cathy Guisewite. Kansas City, Missouri: Andrews, McMeel, and Parker, 1982.

The Dilbert Principle, by Scott Adams. New York: HarperCollins, 1996.

Ellen: My Point... and I Do Have One, by Ellen DeGeneres. New York: Bantam, 1995.

Female Problems: An Unhelpful Guide, by Nicole Hollander. New York: Dell, 1995.

They Used to Call Me Snow White...But I Drifted, by Regina Barreca. New York: Viking Penguin, 1991.

Chapter 18

Friends and Lovers

...I met this guy at UCLA. I wasn't assertive when we met and we discussed the issue. He went to the campus bookstore and looked and looked until he said he found the perfect book for me ~~ The Assertive Woman. We worked the exercises as we read it together."

~~ A twenty-two-year-old college student

We hear from many readers that becoming assertive has had an astounding effect on their relationships with family, romantic partners, and friends. As one person becomes more assertive, the balance of a relationship shifts ~~ sometimes a threatening change. Can we restore balance in our lives, without reverting to the false security of the old ways of behaving? How are women to reconcile the old with the new? Do we push ahead and rock the boat? How can we work through the guilt when we let go of relationships that aren't working? Can the men in our lives participate in this process of liberation for both sexes? How do *they* feel about it?

Being Assertive with Yourself

It starts with you. Being assertive with yourself may be the most demanding relationship of all. You must be comfortable being *alone* with yourself and making your own decisions. As we discussed in earlier chapters, an assertive woman trusts her inner wisdom and bases her assertions on this understanding.

Can you see assertiveness as a way to make room for new choices and possibilities in your life? This is taking a chance on really feeling and being alive! It is the difference between settling for second best, and waking up to new choices that spark adventure and aliveness.

To begin opening up to new possibilities, be truly honest with yourself about any pretenses that you are living. Women who have become masters of deception use assertive skills only to further sabotage themselves or others. An assertive woman answers these questions honestly:

* What am I really committed to?
* What is my payoff or reward for this commitment?
* Is the reward also a punishment, paradoxically?
* Or, does my commitment give me a sense of exhilaration and joy?

If your answers reveal that you are using assertive tools to punish yourself, it is time to let go and make new choices. It is time to become assertive with yourself, to experience your power.

The chart on the next page shows how assertive skills can be used for self-sabotage, or for aliveness and power.

Approaching Mates and Lovers Assertively

> "While reading The Assertive Woman I have been using the exercises to better myself and my personal life. I still find myself in the Compassion Trap with my ex-husband. I'm not going back. I'm going forward to make a better life for me and my children. I'm trying to be assertive, but it doesn't always work and I get depressed. What can I do?"
>
> ---- A data transcriber, divorced and in her thirties

Everywhere women look there are books, magazine articles, advice columns, and talk shows expounding on the do's and don'ts of romantic relationships. The topics range from "how to be a better flirt" by using subtle communication, to the "unconscious attitudes" that separate women and men as two alien cultures.

Other favorite subjects include: the pluses and minuses of dual career relationships (especially the clash between the executive woman and her equally high-powered man); the new "aggressive woman," who asks dinner guests to leave early so that she and her lover have time to make love;

WANTED: DEAD OR ALIVE!!

Dead	*Alive*
Having an assertive discussion with your parents on politics while suppressing your feelings about their constant disapproval of you.	Confronting in a loving way your parents' disapproval and your hurt feelings.
Assertively requesting that your mate correct your child's behavior, while you still feel helpless and powerless to stop the child's manipulations.	Negotiating with your mate how to mutually share the discipline of your child and empower one another to do so.
Telling your date where you'd like to go for dinner and what movie you'd like to see, then feeling obligated to have sex to show your appreciation.	Showing appreciation for your date's cooperation in going along with your plans by inviting him to choose the restaurant and theater next time.
Asserting yourself with a co-worker, but remaining in a job you hate.	Examining your real feelings of dissatisfaction on the job and doing something positive to make a change — perhaps a new job.
Assertively, yet ruthlessly, completing your TO DO list(s) while ignoring messages from your body to slow down, rest, or take a "sanity break"; you are exhausted, irritable or ill.	Being assertive with yourself by listening to your inner wisdom which is guiding you toward balance and harmony in your daily activities.

---

the single woman over thirty who lives with the realities of feminism and the sexual revolution and asks, "Why am I still single?"; the Superwoman who desperately searches for Superman, and for ways to put a little nurturing back into her relationships; the divorcee who wonders how to choose a mate the second or third time around; the partners who wonder how to go from "his" to "hers" to "ours" in a fresh, new way.

How can you make sense out of all of this and make new information work in your own intimate relationships? Recognize that there is no end point where two people can claim that they now "have a relationship," as if it were a goal fulfilled and time to move to the next goal. Relating is a *process* ---- of discovery, of learning and teaching, of giving and receiving, of growing and being, of accepting and challenging. To be assertive with your partner is to live the daily experience of commitment to that process.

Assertiveness in intimate relationships often means risking rejection. Afraid of losing your own identity in love? Working through such fear and conflict can give you the best of both worlds ---- personal freedom *plus* intimacy with a partner.

Approaching Friendships Assertively

"A friend is the highest sense of security one person can experience. With a friend, I can travel the countries of possibility, exploring the limitless boundaries of hope and destination, speaking in only truth: the ultimate language of friends."

A young woman answered a college survey on friendship with this poetic response.

How would you describe your feelings about friendship? Perhaps you reserve friendship for members of your own sex only. An assertive woman has the freedom to enjoy friendships with men as well. The same dimensions of friendship can be shared with them in a non-sexual way.

What about friendships that don't pan out? In her book, *Smart Cookies Don't Crumble*, Sonya Friedman describes a young married woman with children who, in an honest effort to be "true to herself," builds an interior design business. Her friends watch with dismay, anxious that they'll be left out of her life entirely. As a result, they express neither interest nor support: "Their apathy brings tears to your eyes; they make you feel *bad* for feeling good about yourself." Friedman's suggestion is not to *expect* total support when making changes which may be threatening to friends. Instead, rein in your need for approval and emphasize the ways in which your friendships provide a connection.

Confronting their lack of support may terminate or enhance the friendship. In a rapidly changing world, it is common to see friends come and go, to have many acquaintances, and to need close friends more than ever.

When to Let Go

Several years ago, a best-selling poster showed a cat hanging onto a rail, barely keeping itself from falling: the caption read, "Hang in there, baby!" ---- a virtue women are expected to possess. We noticed that women all over the country were congratulating each other for staying in impossible, destructive relationships and situations. Whoever endured the worst for the longest time was admired. That's not assertive behavior — it's the newest form of relationship macho.

An assertive woman knows that making a clean break may be the most assertive act of all. Often, we have little choice about the occurrence of an actual loss: divorce, separation, geographical moves, being fired or laid off from a job, financial losses, or other estrangements. However, an assertive woman can control her feelings, thoughts and reactions. She believes that for every loss, there can be a gain. She embraces the letting go process.

The choice to let go of an unhappy relationship is a vital assertive skill. If you need support in letting go, you'll find some help in the reading list at the end of this chapter. (If the relationship involves abuse, please read the sidebar on pages 60-62.)

The Bottom Line

All relationships — romantic, friendship, family, or professional involve human actions and reactions. They are constantly reverberating to changes in the individuals and their perceptions of themselves and one another. They will never be entirely predictable, measurable or even practical.

The relationship and the people who comprise it cannot be controlled or managed; what is manageable is how you interpret what is going on in the relationship. As we've seen, sometimes it is a choice between "dead" and "alive." Give your relationships your best — and go easy on yourself if it doesn't work out. When you accept yourself, you build the best foundation for relationships that last.

A NOTE ON BEST FRIENDS
by Nancy

In a time when networking and power meals are the preferred means to advance one's career, I long for the fine, out-of-fashion notion of the "best friend." Networks and friendships do sometimes coexist, but the connection to a best friend isn't made because of what may come your way as a result. Best friendships may be downright quirky. But what sweet relief to have a friend who doesn't promise anything more than…well, friendship. With a best friend, you don't have to guess, you know you (and your mistakes and triumphs) are accepted. It's comfortable. It's stimulating.

I've been thinking lately about my best childhood friend: Wendy. We went to school together, played together, devised appropriate torments for our respective brothers, wrote a nine-year-old's version of the ideal cookbook (heavy on hamburgers, desserts, and carrots), shared a passion for building snow-women, taught each other our first ballroom dance steps, stood up for each other, defended each other's characters. For all that, we weren't anything alike: school came easy for me, Wendy had to work hard to get by. I was tall and skinny; she was shorter and stockier. I bit my fingernails; Wendy had the most beautiful hands I'd ever seen. And she was left-handed, a constant fascination to me.

I was invited to accompany her family on summer vacations to the lake — a time I still recall as enchanted. During one such summer at the lake, I found a tiny baby mouse and pleaded to bring it home. Wendy tried to talk me out of it, I remember, saying something about nature and that she didn't think the mouse would survive. I didn't listen; I lined a small box with pink Kleenex and took my mouse home, where it lived for a day. I was heartbroken, but I learned something: I might be smart in school, but Wendy was wise.

Disaster struck some three years later. I moved. We wrote, arranged special and eagerly anticipated long distance calls, sent snapshots and Christmas cards. After a while, the letters dwindled to a couple each year. I didn't see Wendy again until I was a sophomore in college, some ten years later. It was an affectionate and awkward meeting that day, and I think we were both a little relieved when it was time for her to go back to her world and I to mine. We no longer shared a world that belonged to both of us.

Though women are advised to build all sorts of productive relationships, from career networks to marriages, a best friendship carries its own unique rewards. A best friend can get you through ups and downs the way no one or nothing else can. The term itself — best friend — may sound clunky or out of date, but that's a charming dilemma. The effort it takes to kindle and sustain a best friendship is entirely worth your best efforts. If Wendy were here, I'd tell her that.

Suggested Reading

Composing a Life, by Mary Catherine Bateson. New York: Plume, 1990.

The Couple's Journey: Intimacy as a Path to Wholeness, by Susan M. Campbell, Ph.D. San Luis Obispo, California: Impact Publishers, 1980.

Do I Have To Give Up Me To Be Loved By You?, by Jordan Paul, Ph.D., and Margaret Paul, Ph.D. Fine Communications, 1995.

Girlfriends: Invisible Bonds, Enduring Ties, by Carmen Renee Berry and Tamara Traeder. Berkeley, California: Wildcat Canyon Press, 1995.

Just Friends: The Role of Friendship in Our Lives, by Lillian B. Rubin. New York: Harper & Row, 1986.

Keeping the Love You Find: A Personal Guide, by Harville Hendrix, New York: Pocket Books, 1992.

Necessary Losses: The Loves, Illusions, Dependencies and Impossible Expectations that All of Us Have to Give Up in Order to Grow, by Judith Viorst. New York: Fawcett, 1987.

Rebuilding: When Your Relationship Ends (second edition) , by Bruce Fisher. San Luis Obispo, California: Impact Publishers, 1992.

Chapter 19

Assertive Family Relationships

My adventures with being assertive are bewildering my husband of twenty-nine years. My parents are southern and I was raised to leave everything to the MEN and not bother my head, and I found as I raised my five children I was quite capable of taking care of things myself. I am a farm wife and they, traditionally, are the helpmates and take care of the house, plus garden the yard to leave the man of the house to his important work. My parents aren't farmers, so I didn't know some things were my job. Being a farm wife has its rewards, but it's a job you don't understand unless you've experienced it. His work is always more important than yours, but you're expected to have a spotless house, plus always be available for what he wants you to do.

My girls are grown and married. I have one son who I'm trying to teach respect for female ambitions. I have never gone to college --- but I will! I have my real estate license, but not sure I like it.

All my children are supporting me when I take college courses. My husband says he does, but he sure makes it difficult when I have classes. He gets upset at the money going out and wants to know when he's going to get a return on his money.

I'm sure there are more frustrated farm wives out there. There are more and more farm wives working off the farm. The work you do from day to day does not count with IRS if something happens to your husband. All the assets are considered to be his even though you have worked right along with him accumulating them.

Asserting myself is becoming much easier.

---- Letter from a reader in the Midwest

To make room for assertiveness in important relationships, take a fresh look at the state of your relationships. The way we approach relationships as adults was seeded by our interactions with our parents and other authority figures; non-assertive patterns and guilt may have been planted and reinforced early.

When adult difficulties can be traced back to childhood, it's easy to be bitter. Nursing an old grudge, however, prevents us from moving on to discover joy in relationships. To laugh at ourselves and our awkward beginnings, to move forward, we must forgive those who've hurt us.

Mom, Dad and Me

There are hundreds of resources available to help women come to grips with their relationships with their parents (a few are listed at the end of this chapter). How we've interacted with our own mothers and fathers determines in great part how we choose our mates and how we treat children — ours or others'.

Linda Hagood, in *Dawn* magazine, describes three common categories of father/daughter relationships: "Daddy's Girl," "Hands Off," or "Can't Measure Up:"

> The "Daddy's Girl" will remember a father that gave in to her against mom (often not openly, though), and generally treated her as a very special little girl (even after she grew up). Women who experienced "Hands Off" primarily express a sense of their father's absence — either physically or emotionally. They related to and through their mothers because they were a mystery to their fathers. Women who couldn't "Measure Up" often feel competitive with males. Their fathers expected very little success from them because of their sex and yet, they feel a drive to redeem females in the eyes of their fathers.

In her former role as director of a Southern California counseling center, Hagood's counsel to parents and children, urged them to work on their relationships as adults. She believed it possible to complete "unfinished dances" with each parent and move on to assertive ways of relating.

"WHO'S ASSERTIVE?" — A CHECKLIST

Use the following checklist to discover how assertive you allow your children to be, and how assertive you are with them. Each item requires only a "yes" or "no" answer.

* Do I demand from my children only what they can realistically complete at one time?
* When I make requests of my children, do I provide follow-through help?
* In most situations, do my children understand what I expect from them? Are my requests specific as to time, place, and other requirements?
* When I make requests or demands of my children, do I also specify how the demands can be met?
* Do I provide my child with some privacy, or do I feel threatened when I am not in direct control (e.g., talking on the telephone without my knowing to whom she is talking)?
* Do I treat my child as though he has personal rights (e.g., privacy in his own room)?
* Do I set realistic limits for my child (curfew, TV time, household chores)?
* Do I encourage my child to handle some situations independently but with my support (helping with homework, letting her resolve difficulties with friends)?
* Do I allow my child to disagree openly with my judgment (allowing him to choose his own friends)?
* Do I encourage my child to stand up for her rights with others as well as with me?
* When unable to control my child, do I resort to threats, shouting, or physical punishment?
* Do I listen to my child's point of view?
* Does my view always prevail, or do I also let my child "win" sometimes?
* Do I over-protect my child (not wanting him to be involved to be involved in any sports activities for fear of injury)?
* Do I allow my child to state how she feels, without *telling* her how she feels?

After you have completed the checklist, review your responses. Your answers may reflect particular areas that could be handled in a more assertive, less controlling way.

Stepping Out?

An expanding area of concern for women today is how to be an assertive woman within a blended family, one in which there are children from a former marriage. Stepparenting is a unique and challenging role in which you're an authority figure one minute (with support and power assists from your spouse) and an interloper the next! On top of that, stepchildren often exercise considerable power of their own by driving a wedge between the natural parent and stepparent in hopes of keeping the natural parent to themselves and sending the stepparent packing!

The only way to get around this mess is for both parents to decide how to discipline the children, including specific responses to specific problems and what to do if one parent doesn't live up to the deal. Since each parent's wishes are susceptible to manipulation and sabotage by the children, discuss how you can quickly regroup and get back on track. A united partnership doesn't have to limp along as a "broken family."

Assertive Parenting

When you are in the midst of cleaning up spilled milk, officiating whose favorite TV program will be watched, bandaging scraped knees, getting youngsters dressed and undressed, into bed and out of bed ---- acting assertively with them may well be the last thing on your agenda! But if you often feel put upon by your children, you may have brought it on yourself by not taking the reins with them and by not allowing them to learn to act assertively themselves.

We say that as you become more assertive, you will experience the rewards that go along with it. One of those rewards is seeing those around you become more assertive also. As an assertive woman, you are a model for others. Your children, through watching you, can learn to be independent people, and go on to become models for families of their own.

Children, of course, also watch and learn from you when you act nonassertively, and they will learn those behaviors as well. This can have unpleasant results, as it could for Isabel Indirect or Augusta. Isabel's children may learn from her example how to be expert manipulators. Augusta's children may adopt her loud, bossy, and bullying ways to get what they want. And Dorrie's children may learn to be helpless and passive.

Fortunately, children succeed very well in learning to be assertive, and they can learn most of it from you. They will receive the same benefits when they assert themselves as you do when you assert yourself: a feeling of personal worth, strength, and independence.

What attitudes are you teaching your child?

True False

____ ____ Children should be seen and not heard.

____ ____ I spend a good deal of time doing things for my child.

____ ____ I am frequently angry with my child's behavior.

____ ____ My child needs to be protected.

____ ____ My child can make many decisions with my guidance.

____ ____ I encourage my child to do things "for her own good."

____ ____ I feel that my child takes me for granted.

____ ____ My child depends on me for everything.

____ ____ I encourage my child to be independent.

____ ____ I respect my child's feelings and opinions.

You may find that in some situations, you treat your child as a "kid." At other times, you probably see your child as a person, although someone with less personal power than you have. The first step in learning to behave assertively with your child is to recognize she has certain personal rights. It is true that you do have to make decisions for your child's own welfare, but you can also help a child to be assertive and to stand up for herself.

Start by observing what your child actually does and whether it's different from what you *expect* her to do. Usually this means distinguishing between appropriate child-as-child behaviors and child-as-adult behaviors. If you give your child spending money or an allowance, it is unrealistic to expect her to spend the money (or save it) as you would. Part of helping your child to be assertive, then, is to try to avoid expecting her to function as a grown-up. You can then provide support and guidance when it is needed and allow the child to tackle other situations independently.

THE ROCK CONCERT

Cindy, your thirteen-year-old daughter, wants to go to a rock concert in a city twenty-five miles away. It is a week night, and Cindy has school the next day. Several of her friends are going, and one of the parents will drive. You don't want Cindy to go to the concert on a week night, and you are also uncomfortable with the twenty- five-mile distance. Which approach would you choose?

Passive: After listening to her daughter's pleas to go to the concert, Dorrie says: "Oh, I don't know, Cindy. Who is going to the concert? Who is performing?"

Cindy: "All of my friends are going, and there will be lots of bands there ---- I can't remember all of them. Mom, can I go to the concert or not?"

Dorrie: "Well, I don't know; why don't you ask your father?"

Aggressive: Before Cindy is halfway through her request, Augusta interrupts:

Augusta: "Are you crazy? Going to a silly concert on a school night? What's gotten into you?"

Cindy: "But, Mom ---- "

Augusta: "No *buts* about it! Absolutely not! And don't talk back to me like that. If you keep making these ridiculous requests ---- a girl of your age ---- I'll take away your allowance for a week!"

Cindy: "Mom, you didn't even let me explain... "

Augusta: "I said forget it. Don't you argue with me, young lady. You're not going to be there with all those punks, druggies, and who knows what!"

Indirectly Aggressive: Isabel listens to Cindy's request attentively, and then says:

Isabel: "Cindy, you disappoint me. I thought you had better sense. No, not tonight. It's really for your own good. I'm older and I know about the world."

Cindy: "But Mom, everyone's going. It will be fun."

Isabel: "When you're older, you'll see that I'm doing you a favor. It's only that I care about you. Those other parents must not care at all to let their children go. I wish someone had cared more about me when I was a child. You'll be a better person for it, Cindy."

Assertive: Allison listens to Cindy's request attentively, and then replies:

Allison: "Well, Cindy, it does sound like a good concert, and I can see you really want to go, but I'll have to say 'no' this time."

Cindy: "But Mom, all my friends are going! I'll be the only one who will miss it!"

Allison: "I know several of your friends are going. But tonight is a school night and you have to get up early tomorrow morning. I really have to say 'no'. Concerts are fun to go to, and if you were going to a Friday or Saturday night concert it would be okay, but I must say 'no' under these circumstances."

(Or, had Allison not felt ready to let Cindy go to such events at all, her last sentence might have been, "Concerts are fun to go to, but I don't think you are quite ready to deal with such a large event at night just yet. Let's limit it to daytime activities until you are fourteen.")

In this situation, Dorrie was tentative with her "no," and ultimately passed the decision to someone else. Dorrie is more concerned about not displeasing her daughter by saying "no." On the other hand, Augusta doesn't even allow Cindy to finish her request. Augusta barks orders and behaves like a dictator. In this case, Augusta's daughter only had the right to obey. The manipulative Isabel uses an indirect approach with her daughter, by making Cindy feel guilty for even making her request. It is difficult to see how this experience would make her daughter "a better person," as Isabel says.

Allison handles the situation assertively and communicates to her daughter that she has the right to disagree and to bring the subject up again later. Allison doesn't precede her "no" with a lecture, nor does she load Cindy with commands and punishments. Allison encourages assertive communication.

Generally, we suggest you approach acting assertively with children the same way you do with adults. There are two special communication traps to look for when interacting with children: the "Aggression Trap" and the "Slavery Trap." Each can get in the way.

The Aggression Trap

This trap short-circuits assertive communication by forcing an explosion. It generally occurs when you have put off asserting yourself, hoping that the situation will change by itself.

"IT'S MARIJUANA"

Scenario: You suspect that your fourteen-year-old son, Gordon, has been experimenting with marijuana. You haven't mentioned anything to him about it, hoping that it was only temporary. You are hanging up Gordon's jacket one day when a marijuana cigarette falls out of the pocket. You approach Gordon, waving the cigarette in front of him: "I knew it! I knew it all along! Next thing I know you'll be hooked on something stronger! Have you lost your mind? What are you trying to do, land in jail? I can't believe you'd do anything so stupid! Can't you see how dumb you've been? You'll turn into a real addict!"

If you have ever been stuck in the Aggression Trap, you know you feel shaky and angry at yourself for exploding. The trap can be avoided by dealing honestly and assertively with your problems when they appear. Hoping the situation will improve, or merely ignoring it, can build you up for a headlong plunge into an aggressive, irrational encounter.

An assertive intervention would take place as soon as you sense there might be a problem or something to talk about. It might go like this: "Gordon, I want to talk to you about something that's been bothering me lately. I think you might be smoking marijuana, and I'm concerned about it. I'd like to hear your side of it."

The assertive parent acknowledges the child's feelings, and then states clear expectations for the child's behavior. Here's one way to do that:

"I know you want to try marijuana; it's exciting at your age to do something that's 'against the rules.' *I don't want you to smoke marijuana,* and I won't allow you to have it or smoke it here in the house. You're aware of the risks involved, and you'll have to accept the responsibility and the risks if you do use it. You'll be breaking my rules for you, and you'll be breaking the law. I can't support you in that choice; I prefer you didn't use it at all. I know that sounds pretty strong, but that's the way I feel.... Now that you know my point of view, I'd really like to hear yours. It's important to me, and I have as much time as you'd like to talk about it."

In this approach, the expectations, the parent's rules, and the consequences are clear to the child. It is a strong statement, but it allows room for the child to respond.

(Please note that we are not trying to tell you *what* to say in such a situation ⸻ indeed, you may think marijuana use is fine; our purpose is to urge you to give your children clear assertive messages, and encourage them to respond the same way.)

The Slavery Trap

When you perform an endless array of tasks for your children, most of them unnecessary, you are deep into the Slavery Trap. This trap encourages your children to be too dependent on you.

For example, a typical morning finds Dorrie awakening her children for school, bathing and dressing them, preparing breakfast, packing lunches, and driving them to school (only a few blocks away). Realistically, all of these tasks could be performed independently by the children. Dorrie is actually doing her children a disservice by not allowing them to manage their own behaviors. Because they have learned to be too dependent, they won't have the confidence to stand up for themselves when necessary. Parents permit the Slavery Trap at the cost of their child's independence and assertiveness — a high price. Dorrie may also pay a high price as a result of the Slavery Trap. She may grow to resent her children, find that she has little time for herself, and worst of all, once her children are grown, she may realize that her "slavery" was more a burden than a benefit.

Inheriting the Compassion Trap

Parents can pull a child into the Compassion Trap by making her responsible for taking care of her parents' needs. This happens frequently with single parents, who often refer to their child as the new "man" or "woman" of the house. Children resent being placed in this position, but usually do not complain too much because they would feel guilty for saying anything.

A parent who feels helpless can engender a feeling of super-responsibility in a child by forcing him to make decisions or take on adult responsibilities prematurely. The parent may foster guilt in the child as well as excessive compassion. The parent's message is "Care about your parent! Feel sorry for me!"

You know your child is in the Compassion Trap if he says: "Don't worry, I'll take care of you; I'll do that for you, you're too sick; I won't leave you alone." It is understandable that children in the Compassion Trap experience tremendous guilt feelings for pursuing their own interests. They may also develop a tendency to over-protect that sticks with them well into adulthood, when they pass it on to their own children.

Forcing your children to be your "parent" deprives them of their right to choose how they will live. Since the average lifespan is seventy-five years, it isn't too much to let children be children for a decade or two.

In the Land of Giants

Getting your child's attention so you can talk with her is a necessary part of acting assertively with her. Combining several techniques is most effective, particularly with younger children, and also makes you an equal who will talk *with*, not yell *at*, your child.

• Since you are much taller than your (young) child, try bending down so that your child looks down at *you* while you are talking. You can also do this by squatting or sitting on the floor while your child is seated. The goal is to avoid looking like a giant to your child, and to help maintain eye contact, just as you would with an adult.

• Touching your child gently while you are talking ⸺ holding her hand, touching her shoulder ⸺ will help keep your child's attention.

• You can also get your child's attention by saying, "Listen to what I'm going to say, because it's important." Be sure that your voice is loud enough to be heard, but don't unduly raise your voice or threaten. Experiment with your voice volume to find what works best for you. Sometimes keeping your voice lower than normal is the best attention-getter.

Role-playing with Your Child

We believe that the best way to teach your children to be assertive is to act assertively yourself. Since you cannot be with your children all the time, you can teach your children to be assertive by giving them specific instructions, and by "role-playing" ⸺ rehearsing common life-situations ⸺ with them.

Suppose your seven-year-old son, Sean, has a friend who likes to play with matches. Your son tells you that his friend, Tommy, was playing with some matches one day after school, and that he wanted Sean to play with them, too. Your son doesn't want his friend to play with the matches, but he doesn't know how to tell him that. You help Sean handle the situation assertively by pretending to be Tommy. Have Sean practice telling you he doesn't want you to play with the matches ("Tommy, I don't want you to play with matches while you're with me!"). You can give your son encouragement and support for being appropriately assertive ("That's right!" "That's good."), and add suggestions you may have for improvement ("Try saying that again in a louder voice."). You may also switch roles: you pretend to be Sean, and your son takes the role of Tommy.

You can use role-playing with your child successfully to teach assertion. Young children particularly like this approach because it's like a game. By watching you, your son can see clearly how he could handle the situation.

Keep switching roles, and have your child practice a few times more before trying it with a friend.

Behavior Contracting

Another effective approach to encourage assertive behavior patterns with your children is to write a "contract." If both parent and child abide by the terms of the contract, aggressive outbursts and mismanaged communication can be reduced considerably.

A contract clearly spells out what is expected of both parties. Also specified is what each party will receive for sticking to the agreement. Some families prefer to have loosely structured, verbal agreements, while others may choose to write down the terms of the contract. A sample contract is shown below (see *Living With Children* on the Suggested Reading list for more details):

<u>Child</u>	<u>Parents</u>
Complete homework assignments.	Allow child to watch TV after homework.
Do home chores.	Provide allowance.
Tell parents where she is going, when she will be back.	Avoid "nagging."
Do not scatter clothes, possessions around house.	Allow child to keep his room in any condition he wants. Room is the child's personal territory.

Contractual agreements work well for some families, and others prefer not to use them at all. The choice is up to you and your children. If you do decide to try a contract, you must be prepared to follow through on its terms.

An Exercise for Assertive Parents and Children

The following exercise will help assertive parents (and those who are developing assertiveness) to help children grow toward becoming mature, assertive adults.

KING AND QUEEN

This exercise works best with a group of children (at least four and at most ten), approximately seven to ten years old. We designed this exercise to teach children how to give and receive compliments assertively, one of the first steps in learning to be assertive.

The girls and boys in the group take turns being the King or Queen, sitting on the "throne" (a chair placed in the room). The other children and the adult group leader sit in front of the King or Queen as "subjects." The King or Queen calls on subjects individually, and each comes to the throne bearing a "gift" in the form of a sincere compliment for the King or Queen. The children are encouraged to let their imaginations run, and to imagine that the King or Queen is wearing a royal robe, a jeweled crown, and is holding a scepter. As subjects, the children can bow down in front of the throne and present their "gifts," saying, for example, "Queen Susie, I have brought you this compliment: you are fun to be with." The children make eye contact with the King or Queen when they are bestowing their compliments. The King or Queen must acknowledge the compliment in some way, e.g., "Thank you," "I agree with you," "You have pleased me."

The rest of the subjects and the group leader monitor the sincerity of the compliments by cheering or saying "that's good," or by saying "keep trying" or "try again." The children are encouraged to give personal, rather than superficial, compliments. If the compliment is judged by the subjects and adult to be personal ("I like the way you haven't been hitting everyone lately"), the subject receives a reward (fruit, small toy, etc.). If the compliment was thought to be superficial or false flattery ("You're wearing green — that's my favorite color"), the child is encouraged to try again.

The children will lend a great deal of support to each other in this exercise and will offer to help each other out, particularly when a child is having difficulty. (However, you should be prepared to help out if they do not.) This game is really fun for children to try.

The Rights of Small People

The assertive woman recognizes that her children are also people, with rights of their own. She encourages her children to act independently, but also provides specific guidelines for them. When the assertive woman makes a demand or request of her child, she explains clearly what she expects, and how her child can meet her expectations. In return for the child's respect for the home in which she lives, the assertive woman also respects the child's territory. By assertive communication and behavior, the assertive woman avoids the "Aggression" and "Slavery" traps, and avoids passing the "Compassion Trap" on to the child.

If you apply the principles and suggestions in this chapter to your interactions with your children, you will be less likely to terrorize (or be terrorized by) them. If your home has been a constant battlefield, you can look forward to improved communication and, likely, increased peace.

There is no simple, fool-proof formula for living with children, or with anyone else, but the assertive woman is headed in the right direction.

We hope you will include children among the people with whom you will behave assertively. If you'll teach them to be assertive as well, you will be giving them something they can rely on all their lives — a sense of personal worth, strength, and independence.

Suggested Reading

Adult Children of Alcoholics by Janet G. Woititz, Ed.D. Pompano Beach, Florida: Health Communications, Inc., 1990.

It Will Never Happen to Me! Children of Alcoholics as Youngsters, Adolescents and Adults by Claudia Black, Ph.D., MSW. Denver: M.A.C. Publishers, 1981.

Liking Myself, by Pat Palmer, Ed.D. San Luis Obispo, California: Impact Publishers, Inc., 1977

Making Peace With Your Parents: The Key to Enriching Your Life and All Your Relationships by Harold Bloomfield, M.D. with Leonard Felder, Ph.D. New York: Ballantine Books, 1984.

The Mouse, the Monster, and Me, by Pat Palmer, Ed.D. San Luis Obispo, California: Impact Publishers, Inc. 1977.

My Mother My Self: The Daughter's Search for Identity by Nancy Friday. New York: Dell Publishing Co., Inc., 1987.

New Passages: Mapping Your Life Across Time, by Gail Sheehy. New York: Ballantine Books, 1996.

The New Peoplemaking by Virginia Satir. Palo Alto, California: Science and Behavior Books, 1988.

Sister to Sister: Women Write About the Unbreakable Bond, ed. by Patricia Foster. New York: Anchor Books, Doubleday, 1995.

The Stepfamily: Living, Loving and Learning by Elizabeth Einstein. Ithaca, New York: E. Einstein, 1994.

Chapter 20

How Assertiveness Works At Work

*My grandfather once told me that there were two kinds of people:
those who do the work and those who take the credit. He told me
to try to be in the first group; there was much less competition.*

—— Indira Gandhi

Thanks in large measure to the influx of millions of women into the
labor force over the past twenty years, there's been a revolution in
the way we work. The most far-reaching changes were kicked off when
women reminded their employers that it's work *and* family (and
community, and themselves), not work *or* family. They pushed their
companies to find innovative ways to make the most of every smidgen of
talent on their payrolls. In fact, some two-thirds of the professional women
with flexible schedules interviewed by Catalyst, a New York-based
research firm, reported that they would have left their companies had
their requests for nontraditional arrangements been denied. What began
as "women's programs" turned into "work/family initiatives," and now,
so-called "flexiplaces" —— companies that offer flextime, telecommuting,
job-sharing, company-sponsored or on-site day-care —— are becoming the
norm.

As companies warmed up to newfangled work designs, women could
think bigger where their careers (and their lives) were concerned. Today,
women hold top jobs in virtually all corners of the economy, from Wall
Street to Main Street, from pharmaceuticals to the Federal Reserve. They
continue to start their own businesses at a rate three times that of men.
Years ago, a female executive was a rare and unusual specimen; now, as
a friend puts it, "you report to her."

Alas, the picture is not so pretty everywhere:

In *law enforcement*, a pitiful 9 percent of police officers are women, up from 7 percent in 1985. In 1997, only two chiefs of police were women, in Austin and Atlanta.

Under the leadership of Secretary of the Air Force Sheila Widnall (who commands a worldwide force of 600,000), one-quarter of all new *Air Force recruits* are women. But these numbers have grown along with the seamy tales of hazing and harassment of women in every branch of military service.

Nurses, traditionally a feminine stronghold, are now endangered by a new kind of "corporate medicine" that seeks to cut costs by laying them off and replacing them with less-skilled and lower-paid workers. Such restructuring is expected to continue, although the savings are paltry and the impact on patient care is arguably dangerous. Recent studies peg nursing salaries and benefits at about 16 percent of total hospital costs, while health care executives' compensation bloats out of control. According to health care writer Suzanne Gordon, in the mid-90s, compensation for the CEOs of the seven largest for-profit HMOs averaged a staggering $7 million.

Through it all, women just kept on doing what they wanted to do, and so pushed open doors and changed the rules and stomped on obstacles that once barred their way. Whether they own companies or just run them, pound the pavement selling computer innards or cosmetics, or fly fighter jets in formation, working women agree on one thing: assertiveness is a career's most valuable asset. That was true at the three-quarter mark of the 20th century, when the first edition of this book was published, and it's true now, as we enter the 21st. It's how we're going to keep changing the world.

Crafting a Successful Career

When it comes to your work, you can't afford to be passive and you can't afford to step on too many toes ―― unless your first name is Chairman, and even then, people don't forget. You can, however, make a lot of mistakes and survive: Mary Kay Ash, who founded Mary Kay Cosmetics, the second largest direct seller of cosmetics (Avon is number one), once explained that she "failed her way to success." She's in good company: Thomas Edison said the same thing. How do you handle your working life so your mistakes won't derail your progress? We've found the following model very helpful in understanding how successful careers gather steam and keep on going.

Three colleagues looked at the way successful careers progress. They learned that high performance is a matter of performing well in each of four stages: Newcomer, Colleague, Mentor, and Sponsor. At each stage, there are different tasks to carry out, new relationships to forge, and changed expectations. The research showed that the highest performance ratings were reserved for those who were able to keep moving through each stage without getting stuck.

Stage I: The Newcomer

As the new kid on the block, you may be dismayed to learn that management thinks of you as an apprentice, not an authority ---- even though you may have years of prior experience (and perhaps an expensive MBA degree to boot). Your employer is interested in learning whether your judgment can be trusted, observing how well you can perform the basic responsibilities of your new job, and seeing how well you can "get things done" in the organization. Your performance along those lines will be closely watched. Assertiveness aimed at enhancing your own position is likely to be interpreted as premature, naive recklessness now.

Beginnings are delicate times. Maintaining a balance between accepting guidance and demonstrating initiative in your new role is usually the most difficult challenge for the newcomer. The biggest problem you're likely to encounter is the temptation to *oversell yourself*. It's understandable: you want to show you're smart, capable, innovative ---- in fact, all the things success is made of ---- but there is one drawback. If you overfocus on selling your contributions, "you're asking for an audit," as one friend put it. And if you get that audit too soon, you are more likely to fail in a big way, and, even worse, not be given a second chance.

The thing to keep in mind is that you have a job to perform first, and a career to manage (if you want one) second. If you don't do the job well, you won't have a shot at that career. Just "doing the job" can be extremely frustrating, since at this point the work is more detailed and mundane than you probably imagined. Higher-ups expect to guide and direct your work until they feel you are ready for more responsibility and more independence. Personal initiative is welcome, but within clear boundaries established by your supervisor.

This situation irritated a friend who had just been hired into a staff position by a large electronics firm. Convinced she was "management material," she constantly searched for opportunities to demonstrate her organizational skills. Unfortunately, what she didn't take seriously was the way her behavior looked to her peers and to management. So determined was she to showcase her talent that she neglected the nuts and bolts of the job she was hired to do. Higher-ups got the impression that she cared more about moving up than doing her job well. She approached every meeting as an opportunity to assertively state her position, when she should have been listening to what others had to say. As a result, she soon developed a reputation for not being a "team player."

The good news is that she also had a boss who, over several months, took the time to give her feedback about how she was being perceived by those around her. The bad news is that she wanted executive status more: she suspected her boss was simply trying to blunt her otherwise bright career prospects. Eventually, she had alienated too many of the existing management team. The damage was too extensive to repair, and she left the company.

What happened here? The irony is that our friend was doing what women in business have been advised to do — look for ways to stand out, hold your ground, shoot for the top. The problem was that she tried to do all that *too early in her career*. When she should have been learning about her new organization and how things get done there, she overfocused on projecting a "professional" image. She should have listened more and projected less.

Although the emphasis during your first few weeks or months on the job should be on listening and learning, we don't mean to suggest that you should never take an assertive stand when it is called for. The trick, however, is to choose those times very carefully. It is not as simple as some would have you believe.

Are You Sure You Know What "Assertive" Means?

A recent sampling of popular advice on assertiveness on the job yielded this example: You suggest that new product innovations are needed in your company, but the chairman of the planning committee rejects the idea as "blue-sky" and "unrealistic." (Your position relative to the chairman is not clear, but the assumption is that you are subordinate.) The test then offers you three possible responses: 1) lash back at the chairman, citing evidence which supports your case; 2) feel foolish and withdraw from the discussion; or 3) make it clear to the chairman that you expect your ideas and proposals to be given adequate consideration, not be summarily dismissed. The "correct" answer, according to the creators, is the last one ---- supposedly the "assertive" response (as opposed to aggressive and passive).

The problem, however, is that such a recommendation assumes that the organizational landscape is pretty much the same from place to place, and that assertion is assertion is assertion, no matter when, no matter who is sticking up for what they want. The fact, of course, is that assertiveness is a meaningful choice only relative to a particular time and place. What worked in your last job may not fare so well here; what was just right for one organization is foolishness (or worse) in another. Your personal style of assertiveness must be adapted to the situation!

During the early days on the job (and later, too), there is no absolute assertive standard to live up to. Just because you *can be* assertive in a given circumstance doesn't mean you *should be*. If most of the working men and women we know took as gospel the advice handed out in the quiz we described earlier, they would seriously undercut their own credibility. Instead, the best option is ---- usually ---- to learn as much as you can from other's reactions, such as the chairman's pre-emptive response in our earlier example. What could be learned from this outburst? What does it tell you about the organization you have joined? What kind of approach might have been welcomed? How do you feel about your answers to these questions? That's the value in listening to and learning about your organization, your peers, your boss. In the end, only you will be able to judge whether assertiveness was worth it, even whether you have chosen the right company, for the right reasons.

How Can You Find the Right Path?

Appropriate and effective assertiveness on the job isn't always easy to come by. Consider the following experiences:

• You have just taken a job as a sales representative for a hospital supply manufacturer. You have completed the extensive product training courses and know your products ---- and your company's top fifty customers ---- by heart. As you make sales calls, your previous nursing training serves you well. You find you can easily answer customers' questions about how one of your company's products might meet their needs, since your own medical background adds credibility and informed experience to your presentations. You speak with the authority of someone who knows what she's talking about, and your employer has responded enthusiastically to the equipment orders you have worked hard to get.

During the past few weeks, three different customers have described special problems with wound-healing which you feel could be met if your company modifies one of its best selling pieces of equipment. Your experience tells you that their request is not only valid, but could probably be achieved with minor production and design changes. However, when you describe what you see as a new sales opportunity to your boss, she remarks that "All new sales reps want to go along with every customer whim," and she advises you not to pursue the matter further. "You have to do a better job selling what you already have," she says. Should you press for the changes, or sit tight, as your boss advises?

• You are a single parent who joined a large insurance company as an executive assistant six months ago. During coffee breaks and casual conversations with other assistants, you discover there are quite a few other single parents in your division. You have recently spoken with several who complained about your company's lack of support for day care facilities and flexible working hours. You feel strongly that flex time would be a step into the twenty-first century for your company, and you are thinking about forming a task force to begin discussions about flex time and day care. You are aware that the cost of employee benefits and insurance has skyrocketed, but you think you have enough data to show that flex time will actually reduce absenteeism. There are also several firms in your city which have introduced day care on an experimental basis, and have expressed interest in sharing their data with your company. While you believe your case is a strong one, and you have the support and cooperation of half a dozen peers, you are uneasy about how to proceed. You want to handle this situation assertively, and not cave in at the first sign of resistance or become angry and impatient. What steps do you take?

• You are the newest member of the quality control department in your manufacturing company, which makes molded plastic and metal dashboards for automobiles. You care a great deal about your work, and it bothers you to see less-than-perfect parts shipped to customers. Since joining the company, you have noticed a disturbing pattern. Although your boss has stated repeatedly that quality is the most important goal and cannot be compromised, when shipping deadlines are imminent his primary interest is getting the most product out the door as fast as possible. You can understand the pressure to show a healthy number of units shipped at month-end, but you are concerned about the potential for below-par products being built into cars, which seems to you a defeating strategy in the long run. You are sufficiently disturbed by this turn of events to consider taking it up with your supervisor's boss. What is the assertive thing to do?

Each of the three situations might sound familiar to you. In every case, you are faced with a somewhat ambiguous situation in which there may be more than one assertive course: what is appropriately assertive conduct in one organization spell disaster in another!

"OK, Experts, What Are the 'Right' Answers?"

1. The sales rep who wants to make product modifications according to customer specifications faces an interesting dilemma. She could "take the party line," go along with her boss, and offer what sympathy she can to her frustrated customers, stopping short of a further push for the requested changes. If her customers ask her why no product changes are forthcoming, she could rationalize the outcome by blaming it on the slow-moving bureaucracy. This is not an assertive choice, and does not resolve the situation at hand, but is certainly a popular one in many companies! In some organizations, the sales rep could very easily and appropriately go around her boss and take her customers' requests to higher-ups, where they might stand a better chance of being heard and acted upon. This strategy, however, depends on the nature of the organization itself, and won't work everywhere.

Probably the best strategy for the sales rep in this case is to convince her boss to meet directly with a customer or two. The purpose of such a meeting, however, is *not* to sandbag the reluctant boss, but to promote a genuine opportunity to discuss customer service in general. She must also ready both her boss and the customer for such a meeting by speaking with each individual beforehand, when she can answer questions and prepare them for what the discussion might cover. If, however, the boss is still unwilling to meet, the problem extends beyond what the sales rep's assertiveness can accomplish. It will require pressure from senior management to get the boss to take the first step ---- and that's a long way from taking customer suggestions seriously as a way of doing business. The sales rep might be better off finding a company with a clear commitment to customer responsiveness. Going out on a limb to assertively press for more customer contact in the face of such resistance is futile. If she persists, the sales rep will be accused of not being a "team player," and not understanding "how we do things around here."

2. The newly-hired executive assistant who wants to convince her employer to introduce flexible working hours and day care is in a sensitive position. The first thing she should do is get more information. Are the expectations of her peers realistic? Have similar proposals been introduced before? With what results? Is everyone committed to a careful investigation of the possible alternatives, or is this an opportunity to "take a stand?" How willing are the others to be openly identified with the issue? Once she has answered these questions (and it may take some time), she is ready to approach her boss. The object of such a discussion is to briefly summarize the group's position and to obtain feedback that will help put the issue in proper perspective. The assistant herself doesn't want to get stuck as the sole standard bearer in a hot situation: she wants to develop a workable solution that will serve both the company's and the employees' needs. She understands that having her boss's support will be critical. In this case, going to her boss is not giving away her autonomy or power; it's gathering information that is critical to success, and getting it early in the process.

3. The newcomer to the quality control department should first collect information, based on her private observation, of the times in which she believes product quality has been compromised for the sake of expediency. This initial data-collection period will strengthen her when she sits down with her boss to express her understandable confusion about the situation. She should *not* use the information she's gathered as an indictment of her boss's conduct, but as a way to explain why what she sees, on the one hand, and what she hears, on the other, don't fit together. Her next step depends on the results of that discussion. Based on one meeting with her boss and the limited amount of data she's collected, she probably won't have enough information to allow her to take it convincingly to higher-ups. She could instead discuss her concerns with a peer whom she trusts. If she finds agreement, she can raise the issue once again. She shouldn't assume that her boss is acting deliberately; she may discover that her boss is actually unaware of the inconsistency and appreciates the opportunity to do something about it.

The assertive choice is to take it a step at a time, and to make clear that her discomfort arises out of loyalty to her employer, and not from a desire to make her boss look bad. There may, of course, come a time when she realizes that her company attaches less weight to the problem than she does. Indeed, the policy may come from higher up. If that happens, and she feels her own ethics are being compromised, it's time to find a company which is genuinely committed to quality.

Assertiveness in Later Stages: Colleague, Mentor, Sponsor

Once you have completed your career apprenticeship, assertiveness becomes less "loaded," more appropriate, and more productive. Now you'll be expected to show sound, independent judgment, to have an interest in developing others' abilities, and to exercise power and authority directly to influence the overall direction of your company. It's easy to see why assertiveness is so often cited as a leadership characteristic!

Probably the most difficult transition is moving from a dependent position as a newcomer to taking confident independent action as a full-scale team member. There's a great difference in how much power and influence you use in each case. Nothing new there. What may come as a surprise is that leadership is as much a game of inches as your apprenticeship was. Leading means you can mobilize support for a worthwhile goal and sustain it over time. And assertiveness helps not because it will make you a brilliant strategist, but because achieving distinction is a nuts and bolts game.

What's the difference between successful leaders and also-rans? It's not that one has a more brilliantly designed plan than the other. People don't fail because their plans are faulty; they fail because the plans aren't carried out with the same kind of attention that was used to create them in the first place. In the real world, what counts is doing the tiny things very, very well.

A friend runs a little candy company in Eugene, Oregon. Janele Smith's competitive edge against the mammoth chains (who supposedly have the advantage of sheer size) is the superb quality of her products. Fenton & Lee candies are beautiful and original, made with fruits and nuts grown in the Pacific Northwest. Janele would never dream of selling anything but the very best, and she lives that dedication every day so that it is crystal clear to each employee — even the newest. She's nothing short of a broken record when it comes to making the best hand-dipped chocolates around. A less-than-perfect confection has no place in her operation. Janele's strategic secret isn't found in her plans or budgets — it's in her memorable, assertive leadership and skillful, meticulous execution.

Assertiveness on the job, then, is standing up for your department, your product, your company, your reputation, your ideas. There is a certain stubbornness at the heart of really good leadership ---- and followership ---- which comes from the same place as self-confidence, self-respect, and a feeling of power.

Does Your Company Encourage Assertiveness?

We have noted repeatedly in this chapter that assertiveness on the job is, to some extent, in the eye of the beholder. That is, assertiveness will be welcomed in one company and discouraged in another. How can you tell which kind of company you work in? The list of indicators below is intended to give you a head start. Add your own unique observations to it!

Encouraging Signs

Employee suggestions are actively sought in all parts of the operation.

Communication flows openly up, down, and across organizational levels.

Assertiveness is literally rewarded: prizes or other forms of recognition are given for independent action.

More emphasis is placed on performance than on status.

People who speak up are considered imaginative innovators.

Management maintains an "open door policy"; employees need not fear retribution for voicing their concerns or complaints.

Discouraging Signs

Employee participation in policy setting is unheard of.

There are stories about past employees who were fired on the spot for "insubordination."

Your boss does not seem interested in hearing your ideas for improving your department's performance; that's management's job.

You get the impression that employees should be seen but not heard.

Your boss's decisions are capricious and unpredictable.

Morale is low in your department; people feel powerless to make even the smallest change.

Encouraging Signs

Your boss takes the time to listen when you have something to say.

Non-supervisory employees sit on decision-making committees.

Your company or department sponsors regular employee forums where any question is OK.

Your boss regularly asks for your opinion on work-related decisions or issues.

Employee's ideas for new products or services are eagerly sought and the most successful acted upon.

Informed risk-taking (testing a new billing system, streamlining the accounts payable process, modifying an existing product) is the norm.

Being called "outspoken" is a compliment.

Mistakes are regarded as learning experiences.

Your company is fun to work for.

Disagreements are aired openly.

Discouraging Signs

People who even gently criticize company policy are called "troublemakers."

The motto of your group is "Don't rock the boat."

The most frequent words from your boss are, "We tried that last year," or "I'll have to get back to you."

Managers stay in their offices with their doors closed; the only way you can see your boss is to make an appointment.

Yours is a rigid, structured environment in which the newest members are expected to work sixty- or seventy-hour weeks.

There seems to be an excessive amount of politicking and back-stabbing going on.

Most of what you know about your company's plans you learn from the rumors you hear.

Outstanding contributions are not formally recognized.

<u>Encouraging Signs</u>	<u>Discouraging Signs</u>
There are five or fewer layers of management in your company.	Your boss won't back your judgement.
There is a profit or gain-sharing program in effect in your company.	There is no profit or gain-sharing program in which all participate.
Management works to rid the company of excessive rules and regulations, and stresses using common sense in your work.	There is an executive wash-room and reserved parking spaces for executives only.
Flexible work arrangements (flextime, telecommuting, child care) are standard policy.	Management writes frequent memos to announce bad news or make new rules.
All employees are actively encouraged to learn and apply new skills.	Flexible hours are for wimps; it's 9 to 5 or nothing.
Employee development is an investment, funded with at least 2.5% of payroll.	Training dollars go mostly to sales reps and the top brass.
Every year, we review and revise our rigorous code of ethics.	You know who the "hourlies" are, and who is "salaried."
	Ethics? It's whatever we can get away with.

Suggested Reading

America's Competitive Secret: Utilizing Women as a Management Strategy, by Judy B. Rosner. New York: Oxford University Press, 1995.

Breaking the Glass Ceiling: Can Women Reach the Top of America's Largest Corporations? by Randall P. While, Ellen Van Velsor, Ann M. Morrison. Reading, MA: Addison-Wesley Publishing Co., 1994.

Executive Female Magazine, New York: National Association for Female Executives. 800-634-NAFE.

The Language of Leadership, by Dr. Marlene Caroselli. Amherst, MA: Human Resources Development Press, Inc., 1991.

SEXUAL HARASSMENT

When Anita Hill testified at Clarence Thomas's confirmation hearings, women everywhere —– in school, at work, at home —– were reminded that they were not immune to sexual harassment: powerful men could use their status to exploit and intimidate women and get away with it. In spite of a slew of federal and state protections, harassment remains a fact of life in the armed services, in classrooms, on factory floors, and in offices. Although men can be harassed too, women are victimized far more often. A recent study reported that an astonishing 42 percent to 90 percent of working women would probably "experience sexual harassment at some point in their careers."

Legally, sexual harassment means any unwelcome sexual advance (behaviors like touching, pinching, or kissing) or conduct that gets in the way of an individual's performance at work by creating an intimidating, hostile, or offensive environment. When a coworker leaves obscene photographs where you will find them, that's harassment. When a boss makes a job offer, promotion, or favorable performance review contingent on whether you provide sexual favors, that's harassment. And when you're the only passenger in a taxi traveling at fifty miles an hour and the driver suddenly starts yelling and hurling sexual insults at you, that, too, is harassment.

Some women won't report these episodes because they fear retaliation, or because they believe they did something to provoke the harassment. Others keep silent to show they are tough enough to take whatever their coworkers or classmates can dish out. Others just want to forget it ever happened. But if it continues over a long period or is severe, victims suffer from anxiety, lapses in concentration, and physical ailments such as headaches and fatigue. Employers, too, lose productive and motivated employees and their good names in the community.

The first step toward ending harassment is to do something about it. Since managers are bound by law to take action when sexual harassment comes to their attention, it is up to the victim to decide whether to go public with her charges. Obviously, the passive response is to do nothing; she puts up with the torment because she dreads being fired from a job she needs. An aggressive response, in which the victim seeks revenge on her harassers by responding in kind, is to pour gasoline on a bonfire. You can't make a claim of harassment stick when you have escalated the problem. Worst of all, though, is the manipulative employee who charges harassment where clearly there has been none. This sort of maneuver, while rare, sullies every genuine complaint.

To stop harassment, report it: you've got to tell somebody.

• Go to your human resources or personnel department. They administer your company's employee assistance program (EAP). EAP programs are often outsourced ---- an advantage, because it helps to keep things confidential.

• Once you've found the right people, sit down and explain your charges in detail. Bring documentation (names, dates, places, what happened) if you have it. This step matters especially if the harassment has continued over a long period of time.

• Find out what your choices are. What, exactly, is your company's policy on harassment? If you authorize your EAP representative to start an internal investigation, what can you expect when the grapevine gets hold of it? What should your next steps be to protect yourself?

• If you don't like the sound of the answers you're getting, or you want an independent perspective, or your firm doesn't have an EAP, go outside for advice. For starters, look in your local yellow pages under "Women's Organizations and Services," or call your local office of the National Organization for Women (NOW).

Since the mid-90's harassment incidents at Tailhook and Aberdeen, harassment complaints have become legion in every branch of military service. The reporting procedures may vary, so make sure you follow protocol for your branch. If you are in public service ---- teaching or government work ---- you can go to the department designated to handle those complaints, as well as to your union.

The assertive choice is not always an easy one. Even when your company has a formal process for handling harassment cases, protect yourself first. Decide whether you can trust your management or human resources or employee assistance people to keep your complaint confidential. You won't have to worry about this in some companies, but that isn't true everywhere. If you are concerned about privacy, you can seek objective counsel outside your company. Then you can go ahead with an internal investigation, or one conducted by a third party. Depending on the specifics of the case ---- when there is a claim of physical assault or rape, the harasser may face criminal charges ---- you may be able to file a complaint through state and federal venues as well.

Chapter 21

The Mythology of
The Working Woman

Being a career woman is harder than being a career man. You've got to look like a lady, act like a man, and work like a dog.
— Margot Kidder

Although more than half the women in America work, there are few places — from inner city hospitals and gritty assembly lines to the rarefied air of universities and uptown law firms — in which women feel truly welcome. Even a woman who is fully credentialed and qualified will, sooner or later, bump into an unprinted code that says she lacks the requisite confidence (not to mention the *cojones*) to perform, that whispers she's an invader who must be driven out. It's all part of the persistent mythology of the working woman.

Whether she's a senior member of management or the newest teacher's aide, no working woman is completely immune to the sting of these particular slings and arrows. In this chapter, we'll take a look at five hallmark myths: *the Too-Emotional Woman; the Insecure Woman; the Workhorse Woman; the Unprofessional Woman;* and *the Superwoman.* They are unique to working women and have nothing at all to do with fairness or observable job performance; nonetheless, each of the myths has the power to derail a career or short-circuit a job well done.

The presence of women in increasing numbers is still a new development in American business, even in fields which traditionally have attracted them: public relations, personnel, fashion, retailing, education (teachers more often than administrators), health care (nurses more often than physicians). Yet women are expected to prove themselves worthy of their job responsibilities in ways not demanded of men. It's even harder on women who have broken into exclusively male conclaves —— airline pilots, scientists, high-flying financiers, dentists. Women must prove, among other things, that their "raging hormones" will not cloud their decision-making ability, that they will not crumble in the face of criticism, that they can handle "adult responsibility," that self-confidence and strength are not uniquely masculine characteristics.

We describe each myth, show how it can affect the way a woman is perceived in her job, and then debunk it! Part of being assertive on the job involves doing much the same thing —— learning to spot the myths that affect your job performance and progress, and assertively sweeping them away. Don't assume that every roadblock in your job is your fault, or that any difficulties you encounter are of your own making, or that everyone is against you personally. We think the five myths bring some perspective to a hotly debated issue.

THE MYTH OF THE TOO-EMOTIONAL WOMAN

Those with a hankering for this ubiquitous myth contend that a woman is poorly suited for positions of significant responsibility (power) because she will panic under pressure (and therefore cannot be counted on in a crisis), will crumble or explode if criticized, cannot stomach confrontation, and generally allows her heart to overrule her head. The old logic is inescapable. To hold on to her career she must exercise judicious control over her nine-to-five emotions (to do less, of course, would be reacting like a woman instead of thinking like a man).

But the office, argues Dr. Irene Pierce Stiver, director of psychology at Boston's McLean Hospital, has always been emotional territory. "Women give men permission to be intensely emotional. Men can be angry, vengeful, fiercely competitive —— these are all emotions." But giving men the go-ahead to rant and rave doesn't guarantee women the same privilege. The woman who shows anger or admits she has career plans is scorned —— a barracuda, something predatory, with teeth. She is admitted to "people" functions, owing to her more sensitive nature, but barred from others for the same reason.

Emotional Management Works: When learning the ropes of corporate politics, maintaining professional reserve and keeping a lid on one's emotional life may be well-spoken advice. But when the issue is productivity, distinguished performance, and extraordinary leadership, the operative words are ownership, commitment, and caring ---- conspicuous in all corners of exceptional organizations, sadly lacking in the also-rans, and emotional as all get-out.

Traditionally, women employees have been regarded as the keepers of the emotional flame in their companies. When found in men, that emotionalism is often respected as company spirit, but in women, it's a sign of weakness. It's still the department secretaries who make sure birthday cards go out, one of the few approved emotional expressions for many working women. At the same time, what might be the assertive expression of frustration with friends doesn't translate as such in the office. The secretary who complains to her associate that "I can't stand it when Ms. Jones gives incomplete directions," or "It drives me crazy when Mr. Thompson wants me to tell callers he isn't in the office when he is," is clearly communicating her frustration, but such commonplace expressions only diminish her effectiveness. When an emotional response is sparked by impatience, for example, it is usually read as weakness, not strength ---- in both women and men.

But when emotion accompanies strength ---- rallying support to meet a deadline; expressing clear, firm support for a desired change; mobilizing a group to improve its work performance ---- the emotional component is not only helpful, it is essential.

The irony, of course, is that this new approach depends on the same characteristics that women have been advised to abandon for the sake of their careers. Look at the people who have built great businesses during the last couple of decades; they're overtly emotional. They care about these businesses of theirs, and they emphatically do not owe their success to a cool, numbers-only rationality. Think of Anita Roddick, who could not have launched The Body Shop and made it thrive over two decades unless she hustled like crazy chasing her goal and refused to stop until she had mowed down every barrier in her way. Ditto Bill Gates at Microsoft, and Ruth Owades, who started Calyx and Corolla (an upscale fresh flower mail-order business). The truth is that analytical talent is never enough; it takes real passion to build a business, as every entrepreneur knows.

THE MYTH OF THE INSECURE WOMAN

Women have been told that they lack the confidence they need to perform successfully on the job. "She's insecure." "She waffles on decisions." "She doesn't trust her own judgment." "She's not tough enough." This is the stuff the myth is made of; its corollary is that women believe it. Convinced we are our own worst enemies ---- and finding ready agreement on the part of some male bosses or peers ---- we invest countless hours and a good deal of money to make ourselves over into worthy competitors for better jobs.

When *The Assertive Woman* was first published, it spawned some forty books on the same subject; assertiveness training seminars appeared in the course catalogs of almost every university, community college, or women's resource center in any city you could name. Believing that the reason for our dismal prospects "lay in (our) own psychology," according to Professor Rosabeth Moss Kanter of Harvard's Business School, women literally flocked to the programs in hopes that our underlying deficiencies would be fixed.

Later, women were advised how to dress for success, and, most recently, how to dress in our most becoming colors. When management's doors failed to open for assertive, well-dressed women, it was taken as proof of our persistent personal shortcomings.

We were too busy learning how to pull ourselves up by our own bootstraps to notice the inherent fallacy in such an endeavor. Organizations seemed no more receptive ---- and perhaps less so ---- to self-improved women than they were to the original variety! If women are to have a real shot at the jobs and careers they want, it is the organization ---- not its women ---- that could use the overhaul.

New Environments for Women ---- and for Men: The tight-fisted control typical of rigid, top-down organizations is giving way to hands-off, open-book management, which makes everyone responsible for creative contributions and grants them the elbow room they need to do it. Headquarters is just a place where the invoices are printed; the real work is done out in the field or on the factory floor. A few who get it right:

$800-million W.L. Gore & Associates, makers of GoreTex™ breathable fabric, has long been famous for its "lattice organization," which resembles the lattice structure of a crystal molecule. There is no fixed authority in the traditional sense; the company runs on fairness, freedom, commitment, and a precept called "waterline," which spells out the responsibility of each associate to consult with other associates over issues critical to the company's overall health. There are, natch, no formal titles at Gore (other than the ubiquitous "Associate") except for one "Supreme Commander," conferred on one long-time associate who held it until she retired.

The story is different at Oticon, a Danish company founded in 1904 as a family firm and once the world's largest maker of hearing aids. Between 1980 and 1990, the company got sleepy; it didn't keep pace with the competition, and lost fully half its market share. The company's leadership were convinced they had to innovate or die.

Eye-popping changes swept the company. Every reporting relationship was eliminated, along with formal job descriptions; employees had absolute permission to pursue objectives the way they saw fit. Meanwhile, the company moved into a totally open office plan ---- no walls, dividers, credenzas, or desks. Each employee was given a cart on wheels, and could move around at will to work on what needed to be done. They dubbed their invention the "spaghetti organization," where formal departments, job descriptions and routines were replaced by fluid, flexible projects. As people took on multi-job assignments, they stopped thinking of themselves as narrow, one-note specialists.

Performance improved dramatically: Oticon regained most of its share against competitors and cut its product development time in half. They credit their company credo, "Cogitate Incognito," (Latin for "Think the Unthinkable") for the inspiration to break old rules and try totally new ways of doing things.

You could well argue that women have an upper hand in places like these, where the emphasis is on performance, not politics, and nontraditional measures proliferate, such as tracking the degree to which a leader contributes to others' development.

Do Nice Girls Finish Last? Working in one of these new organizations asks a lot of a person. When you stop and think about it, you can see why you have to do more ---- a lot more ---- than show up. In *Why Good Girls Don't Get Ahead...But Gutsy Girls Do*, Kate White (editor-in-chief of *Redbook*), reveals nine secrets every modern career woman needs to know. Having once been a "good girl" (a phrase chosen deliberately because of the instant reaction it provokes and the fact that women have heard it a million times during their lives), White explains that "inside most good girls, there's still a spirited, adventurous, bubble-blowing, puddle-jumping, hair-scalping girl biding her time. When your face aches from smiling too much or your stomach hurts after a pathetic raise, it's just a signal of the tension from trying to keep her buried." Here are Kate's "good girl" and "gutsy girl" profiles, side by side.

A good girl ...	_A gutsy girl ..._
1. Follows the rules	1. Breaks the rules, or makes her own
2. Tries to do everything	2. Has one clear goal for the future
3. Works her tail off	3. Does only what's essential
4. Wants everybody to like her	4. Doesn't worry whether people like her
5. Keeps a low profile	5. Walks and talks like a winner
6. Waits patiently to get raises and promotions	6. Asks for what she wants
7. Avoids confrontations	7. Faces trouble head-on
8. Worries about other people's opinions	8. Trusts her instincts
9. Never takes risks	9. Takes smart risks

In the new workplaces, there is no question that "gutsy girls" are the movers and shakers, the ones who make things happen. Professional achievement and success eludes "good girls," and seeks instead those who transform themselves into gutsy ones ---- or, as we know them, assertive women.

THE MYTH OF THE WORKHORSE WOMAN
(or, "Women must work twice as hard as men to be thought half as good")

Author Marilyn Loden in her book *Feminine Leadership*, recounts this tale: "At a mock graduation ceremony for twenty women in training to become service technicians, certificates of achievement were awarded to everyone who had completed the rigorous ten-week course. The inscription on the award read: 'Whatever women do, they must do twice as well as men to be thought half as good. Fortunately, this is not difficult.'" Working women in every industry agree with Loden when she asserts that they must work harder than men to succeed.

Exploiting the "Worker Bee" Syndrome: There are, of course, organizations which ferociously exploit women's willingness to work hard. They use women to get the job done, because they know we are great worker bees. There may be no money and no recognition in it, but women do it to prove we're capable and independent. Sometimes, what we're really showing is that we can be intimidated.

What we believe we are doing with our overachieving ways is putting to rest the belief that women aren't tough enough to handle a job. The strategy is only partly successful. Plain hard work is seldom recognized, earning women no more than "assistant vice president" or "acting vice president" titles --- but no shortage of responsibility or extra hours.

Hard work is not all bad, of course. When organizations recognize and reward outstanding effort ---- real meritocracies ---- dedicated contribution is the truest source of extraordinary performance. More than one business has been started, though, because their founders had big dreams --- dreams they could not fulfill in big companies, no matter how hard they worked.

Thousands of women have resolved the work-till-you-drop question by learning what they do best, deciding what they're willing to give up for the sake of their work (or dream), and researching what companies to stay away from. It takes real guts to do what you know in your heart you can do, whether it's refusing to be overworked and undervalued by an employer, or going out and building a business and rewriting the rules to suit you. Take care with the choice.

THE MYTH OF THE UNPROFESSIONAL WOMAN

A long time colleague and national director of the National Association for Female Executives, Wendy Reid Crisp described (as only she can) a certain encounter on a rainy Monday morning as she tried to hail a taxi. Competition for a ride is especially fierce. Loaded down with overstuffed briefcase and bulky manuscripts, she cannot gracefully assert her place in the taxi queue outside Grand Central Station. After several others push and shove their way past her, Crisp realizes she'll have to give this competition all she's got. Deciding that "total imperialistic aggression is called for," she dashes at a vacant cab just as a man in a Burberry raincoat makes his approach. She gets there first. She clings to the door handle, won't give it up. Crisp recounts his response: "Oh, very nice. Very ladylike." And then, he adds a final insult. *"Very professional."*

That story rings bells for any woman who has ever run into the limits of professional behavior. "What is 'professional' conduct keeps you in your place. 'Unprofessional' used to be called 'immature.' But if a woman ---- say a director of marketing ---- does things differently from the man who had the job before her, she's unprofessional. If I did the same things as my male counterpart might ---- he's an 'outrageous genius,' but I'm unprofessional."

The rather Victorian "unladylike" has been replaced by the modern "unprofessional," but the song, as they say, remains the same: It means she's stepped outside traditional, acceptable bounds; she's forgotten her proper place.

Professional conduct has to do with honorable behavior, treating people with respect, not going back on your word, doing the best you can, refusing to sell trade secrets to the other side ---- but it is not necessarily unprofessional to exhibit poor judgment ("That's what people do when they're not forty years old yet," says Crisp); to make a mistake; to expect others to honor the terms of a deal; and it is not unprofessional to violate some "mythical pecking order," in Crisp's words. But to be summarily dismissed with a hissed "how unprofessional" ---- now that's low.

A Woman's Proper Place: But even 21st-century professional women are expected to remember their proper place ---- which, according to some, is limited to service businesses and "people functions," areas where they can make full use of their feminine intuition, sensitivity, and desire to nurture others. People functions, and the jobs within them, however, are not accorded the same respect as line or operating jobs, where the emphasis is placed on the task, the bottom line, and profit and loss.

Crisp warms to this subject. "Women are regarded as intuitive right-brainers who cannot deal with hard data or acute analysis," she declares. "Intuition is neither accepted nor admired in business. The dominant belief is that women are too emotionally attached to people to function objectively; they're afraid to deal with budgets or numbers." Corporate America has acknowledged women as good nurturers. At least they told us we were good at something! Yet women are still the ones ---- regardless of the seniority of their positions, in many cases ---- who are expected to order the office birthday cakes and keep track of births and anniversaries.

Women, in other words, have their own special slots in which they must demonstrate competence and comfort, and which are far removed from the mainstream of the business. Those who succeeded in non-traditional areas did so by proving their "bottom line orientation."

This is an area in which educational programs designed for women can provide a needed service. But ask a professional woman if she participates in all-women educational or special interest groups today and she'll likely tell you, "Oh, no. I outgrew all that years ago. Women's groups are passe." Women's groups may be good for an evening's entertainment, but we reserve our respect for the co-ed variety. In our haste to avoid being labeled "troublemakers" or "radical feminists," we have cut ourselves off from a powerful source of information and support, from organizations and programs that have moved mountains for many.

The nature of women's groups and programs has changed over the last decade; they offer positive solutions, not a chance for catharsis. They provide the chance to learn some new skills without an unwanted, judgemental audience; they also teach concrete, useful skills in financial management or planning that some women prefer to learn outside their own organizations, on their own time. It's a lot easier to relax and not worry about asking a "dumb" question when you are among friends.

THE MYTH OF THE SUPERWOMAN

Quick, see if you can name five women who have it all, do it all, and never even break a sweat.

Give up? You're not alone. Doing and having it all is a very pretty image, the super-successful woman with a magic touch, whose many responsibilities to employer, community, friends, kids and car pools exhilarate rather than exhaust. But that image sold us out, and we hardly noticed. It says that doing it all is as easy as walking and chewing gum at the same time, if you're a real woman who has her life together. Lesser vessels need not apply.

To protest that it's not easy, that it's agonizing to make the right professional and personal choices is to miss the point entirely: Most of us work because our families depend on our paychecks, and not out of a smoldering need to prove there's nothing we can't do. We like our jobs, we might even love them --- but trade-offs are mandatory.

In *Our Wildest Dreams*, author and business owner Joline Godfrey believes that tough as it can be, "making the necessary trade-offs... enables us to create businesses that adapt to our needs rather than continuing to build businesses that force us to adapt to ill-fitting conventions."

Companies are seductive. To fend off "the call of traditional cultural values regarding what we 'owe' to work," Godfrey presents a roster of questions that businesswomen she knows have asked themselves. The process of imagining and choosing among many possibilities is a powerful talisman against Superwomanhood, because it never lets you forget you have to make a real decision about what matters to you. Here is Joline's list, the first step toward designing a business (or a career) that gives you what you want:

* Do I want meaning? What meaning?
* Do I want to grow, explore, and discover?
* Do I want to devote all, some, or most of my life to this effort?
* Do I want to work with a few or a lot of people?
* Do I want to make a difference?
* Do I want to do this alone?
* Do I want to have fun?
* Do I want to create an environment within which others can have fun, too?
* Do I want to be richer than Midas?
* Do I want to have time with family and friends?

There is one new and provocative twist in this tale. A British newspaper columnist, Neal Ascherson, hit it on the head when he argued that "if you want to see the future of work in the 21st century, you should ask your mother." He meant that as work becomes more and more flexible (fluid schedules, looser structures, multiple projects running at once), mothers have the new "right stuff" for 21st-century business. They are old hands at juggling a menagerie of things at the same time, as Ascherson notes: "Here is a woman buttering two scones, crossing the kitchen to pick up a fallen child, buttering another scone, answering another knock on the door... rearranging a cupboard shelf, going for the last sheet left on the line." Women who juggle work and family succeed by operating on several different levels simultaneously. It's a way of saying that women do have it all — the right skills and instincts, everything it takes to run a business, a home, a business at home — you name it.

The rules of business are being rewritten. Working women are rethinking how and why they do what they do, questioning old patterns and assumptions, and sometimes inventing brand new enterprises on a foundation of fresh ideas. Such clarion sentiments paint a different picture (and an assertive one) than the woman who is enslaved by her job and the nonstop demands of friends and family. As Joline Godfrey says, it isn't "work, work, work" anymore. It's "work, live, love and learn" that counts.

Suggested Reading

Balancing Act, by Joan Kofodimos. San Francisco: Jossey-Bass, Inc., 1993.

The Education of a Woman: The Life of Gloria Steinem by Carolyn G. Heilbrun. New York: Ballantine Books, 1996.

Executive Female magazine, the official publication of the National Association for Female Executives. For membership information: 1-800-634-NAFE.

Inc. Your Dreams, by Rebecca Maddox. New York: Penguin USA, 1996.

Our Wildest Dreams: Women Entrepreneurs Making Money, Having Fun, Doing Good, by Joline Godfrey. New York: HarperCollins Publishers, Inc., 1992.

Success and Betrayal, The Crisis of Women in Corporate America by Nehama Jacobs and Sarah Hardesty. New York: Franklin Watts, 1986.

Talking from 9 to 5, by Deborah Tanner. New York: William Morrow and Co., 1994.

Why Good Girls Don't Get Ahead... But Gutsy Girls Do, by Kate White. New York: Warner Books, Inc., 1995.

Women Incorporated magazine, Sacramento, California: 1-800-930-3993.

Women's Wire, a lively and comprehensive internet site just for women, at http://www.women.com

Working Woman magazine, New York: 1-800-234-9675.

Chapter 22

The Hardy Spirit

"1,952 BULLDOGS AND 1 BITCH."
---- Message emblazing the T-shirts of Shannon Faulkner's
all-male classmates at the Citadel.

Janet Reno, attorney general. Sally Ride, astronaut. Shannon Faulkner, first female Citadel cadet. Sherry Lansing, Paramount Studios chief. Bessie Coleman, first African-American aviator. Linda Wachner, head of retailing jewel the Warnaco Group. Barbara Walters, TV journalist. A working mother of three in North Dakota.

What do these women share? We call them "hardy spirits," people who every day conquer fatigue, fear, disappointments, tough times, even danger. Maybe it's because they adhere to Linda Wachner's favorite maxim: "Do it now." Or maybe they just don't know any other way except straight ahead. Whatever their reasons, they are all women who, given a chance, we would want to know better.

Whether you find them in Calcutta or Bismarck or a thousand places in between, these are women who count on themselves, who have learned to listen to and respect their own opinions; women who stand by their own perceptions and who are willing to act on them. They aren't always cheerful, but they are, somehow, optimistic. They expect good things from themselves. They believe they can handle what life gives them, and they know they can make the kind of life they want. They will take a few chances.

The pessimistically inclined, on the other hand, have no more faith in themselves than they have in anyone else. When the spouse does not run off with the neighbor, they are amazed. If the new venture fails, or every day is not a holiday, the cynic cannot be accused of lack of faith, but merely of realism when she says she told you so.

But let's make this clear at the beginning: a hardy spirit is not necessarily the one smiling out from the cover of *Time*, the one who takes such bold, audacious steps that you cannot imagine yourself doing the same in a million years. To cultivate a hardy spirit is not to aim for flashy, eye-catching gestures of bravery. It is not grandstanding or making bet-your-career decisions, nor is it aiming to please. The hardy spirit begins with a certain calm determination, a vision of where you are headed, bolstered by the faith that you can get there. The rest is accomplished in tiny, tiny ways: taking advantage of the opportunities you see, making the most of the skill you have, discovering that you can tolerate (and learn from) the unpleasant or uncomfortable, that disappointments can be bridged, and never, ever giving up.

We could each make our own lists: "Hardy Spirits I Have Known (or Wish I Knew)." Women who, from Kansas City to Hollywood to Johannesburg, share that same quality of rootedness, bravery —- even boldness —- in the face of difficulty. It is impossible to imagine such women scurrying away from trouble or challenge. They take things as they come, bit by bit, step by step, even when a single step seems more like a leap off the edge, when safety or common sense might dictate hanging back.

If we ever build a Hardy Spirit Hall of Fame, Elaine Chao will have a special alcove. When the 110-year old United Way of America was in free fall after a sordid scandal involving its former president William Aramony, it was Elaine Chao who turned it around. Chao, a former Peace Corps director, stepped into an organization that suffered deeply from strong competition for donor dollars, declining contributions, a weakening economy, and disillusioned customers.

Chao acted quickly to initiate radical reforms in business conduct, management practice, governance, and fiscal accountability. She trimmed headquarters staff by a third, opened the United Way's national governing board to include local United Way chapters, and together with her staff crafted a formal code of ethics. Knowing that she embodied hopes along with doubts about the future of the United Way, in her first year Chao met face-to-face with customers, contributors and local volunteers in communities in twenty-six states ––– and got an outraged earful. But she saw their anger as a positive sign, believing that people would not react so strongly unless they really cared about the charity's future.

Just shy of four years after her arrival, Chao resigned to pursue political and public policy interests. She leaves behind an invigorated, restored United Way. Her gutsy moves brought an organization back from the brink, and made it possible to change old ways of thinking and to concentrate on the future of philanthropy and the health of American communities.

Hardy spirits can be found anywhere. In Hollywood, Penny Marshall became the first woman director to break $100 million at the box office (*Big*), an accomplishment she would repeat three years later with *A League of Their Own*. You cannot deliver what Marshall has without substantial reserves of inner fortitude.

Barbra Streisand also ranks up there in the directorship sweepstakes; *Prince of Tides* pulled in about $74 million. Still revered for her incomparable voice, Streisand's "The Broadway Album," a collection of classics, is a musical object lesson in perseverance and developing a hardy spirit. Finding little encouragement for such a project, Streisand doggedly pursued her vision until it was real; she even found a song which captured the whole process, and then persuaded Stephen Sondheim to write additional lyrics to express her experience.

And it's not just the rich and famous. All across the country there are women who are up with the sun every day, getting little fingers into mittens, dishing out breakfast, holding down jobs, making house payments, contributing to their communities. They may be the hardiest of spirits: the women who will never have public accolades, but who deserve them nonetheless.

It would be easy to conclude that the hardy spirit takes a highly public stand against things as they are, but it is not true. Small, private stands count, too. Everywhere there are women who bring their intelligence and stamina to benefit their kids' classrooms, their communities, their families, and themselves. And most important, inside each of us is plenty of kindling to spark the hardy spirit, which is just waiting for a reason to show.

The hardy spirit can be encouraged, coaxed forth. You don't need a happy childhood (some would say that overcoming a bad one makes for the hardier spirit). You don't need a certain education. The sort of equipment you will need can't be bought: courage, and a fine sense of humor. The essence of a hardy spirit is some measure of each.

Courage: Where would the assertive woman be without that? Every day we're handed dozens of chances to step out and see what we're made of. Philosopher Paul Tillich once wrote that "courage is the knowledge of what to avoid and what to dare." The operative word is "knowledge," and the key is choice. Taking up every dare that comes your way isn't courage, it's recklessness. The courageous take smart risks; they know what they're getting themselves into. They are alert to the possibility that marriage becomes divorce, but they know themselves and their partners well enough to say, this is worth it.

The thing about people with courage is they actually practice it, every day, to know how it feels and to recognize danger signs. They can see themselves bouncing back from disappointment or worse, where the timid, once burned, never try again. A mix of ingenuity, inventiveness, and action marks the courageous individual.

Practice, Practice, Practice

When you embark on a learning adventure — such as becoming an assertive woman — your skills might seem old and stale, and things that could always hold your interest have lost their allure. You are changing, and your skills and knowledge haven't caught up to you yet. This is the perfect time to move from thinking about being more assertive and actually road test new ways of doing things. No need to put your whole life on the line. Here are some suggestions that all contain elements of hardiness. Choose some to try:

* Sign up for the piano/violin/ukulele/singing lessons you always wanted to take.
* Next time you're in a restaurant, order something you've never had before.
* Face Americans' biggest fear head-on: enroll in a public speaking course.
* Next time you suffer a disappointment (a crushing defeat, even), don't whine and don't complain. Imagine how Katharine Hepburn would handle it. Do likewise: "Hepburn" it.
* Wear red.
* Write a letter to the editor of your local newspaper about a topic that is important to you.
* Join an exercise class.

* Forgive the one who done you wrong.
* Every day this week, look for a chance to say, "why not?" when somebody tells you something cannot be done.
* Watch a scary movie all the way through. (We offer this seriously, but advisedly: Nancy still refuses to watch *Psycho*.)
* Become a Big Sister and spend time each week with an underprivileged child.
* Learn to swim.
* This week, say "no" to three requests.
* Ask a friend out to dinner.
* Ask somebody that question you've been dying to ask.
* Volunteer a few hours each week at your local hospital, AIDS charity, hospice, or deliver Meals on Wheels.
* Try an "Outward Bound" weekend program.
* Give a speech.
* Take a vacation by yourself --- even if it's only a couple of days.
* Move your desk.
* Learn to speak another language --- Spanish, French, Italian, Russian --- or maybe Windows 95 or HTML.
* Adopt a puppy or kitten, or sweet older animal.
* Keep a journal, and write in it every day.
* Every hour today, take a three-minute break.
* Find out how to "surf the Net" and discover e-mail.
* When was your last complete physical exam?
* Go to your high school class reunion.
* Tomorrow, spend your lunch hour in a totally new way.
* Read those books you thought were garbage in high school.
* Be the first to laugh at a joke; don't hold back to see if somebody else is laughing first!
* Get up early and go for a run or walk.
* If you supervise others at work, ask them what three things you do that they appreciate, and what three things drive them crazy. Listen! Take what you hear seriously, and begin to mend your ways. Repeat this process once a month.
* To a good friend, admit the truth.
* Volunteer to do something you wouldn't normally do (organize a conference, make a birthday cake, sit on a task force).
* This weekend, do something new.

* Watch a funny movie about assertive women and hardy spirits: How about *The First Wives Club* or *A League of Their Own?*
* Spend an uninterrupted hour with your kids ---- nothing flashy, just enjoying their company.
* Let your boss know when you think she's done a good job.
* Write a thank you note.
* Get that high school diploma, or college degree.
* Next time something makes you angry, admit it and get it off your chest. Don't pretend your feelings aren't important enough to express.
* Clean out your closets.
* Take a different route to work or school in the morning; what have you been missing?
* Take a stand.
* Get to the point where you can recognize the earliest signs of stress in yourself. Push yourself to reach a cherished goal, but honor your limits.

To step toward becoming an assertive woman is to move toward courage: to say no, offer a compliment, declare your love, make a mistake, visit the dentist or change your mind. What makes each step possible is the faith that you can handle the consequences. If you think of each entry in your Assertive Behavior Hierarchy as a lesson in courage, you have your very own design for a personal learning adventure. Practice makes it easier ---- and funnier. The hardy spirit laughs at herself and her trials and tribulations. Humor reconciles otherwise impossible situations and is sometimes the only thing that keeps disappointments and setbacks from overwhelming us.

The hardy spirit ---- a special blend of strength, vulnerability, and fun ---- lives in us all. Get to know her.

She's worth it.

Suggested Reading

Body and Soul: Profits with Principles, by Anita Roddick. New York: Crown Publishers, 1991.

Chicken Soup for the Soul: 101 Stories To Open the Heart and Rekindle the Spirit, by Jack Canfield and Mark Victor Hansen. Deerfield, Florida: Health Communications, Inc., 1993.

Sequencing: Having It All but Not All at Once... by Arlene R. Cardozo. New York: Macmillan, 1989

Chapter 23

The Most Often Asked Questions About The Assertive Woman

Yeah, but can she cook?
—— Overheard in a bookstore

The *Assertive Woman* sparked questions right from the start. Over the past twenty years, we have heard from hundreds of readers —— and have ourselves worked with thousands more women and men —— who, with the assertive assist of this book, found their own voices and the courage to speak their minds. In letters from art critics and librarians, programmers and soldiers, readers told us about their triumphs and letdowns, insights and understanding. They had different backgrounds and talents, but their questions were consistent. Here, we answer the questions we are asked again and again.

Although your book presents four behavior types, it seems that assertive is the only right one. True? We think so, because its encourages self-respect —— a difference that distinguishes it from the passive, aggressive, or indirect approaches. Somebody always seems to be the loser in those exchanges. Since it entered the American mainstream more than twenty years ago, assertiveness has appealed to women who felt powerless and invisible —— women who wanted to call the shots for a change, to say "no," and to stop apologizing every time they turned around. An assertive reply was such a relief. As always, it is up to you to decide if and when to assert yourself. Sometimes you press your advantage, and sometimes you walk away, but if you make the choice honestly and can live with the consequences, don't worry whether what you did was the assertive thing. You've done the best you can, and that's what counts.

Are you saying there are times when passive, aggressive, or indirect approaches are better? It's more a question of timing than technique. You will run into certain predicaments that can't be dispatched quickly or easily. A complex or lengthy negotiation, for example, requires give-and-take (sometimes more give and sometimes more take) and a series of discussions. Common sense calls for flexibility — taking a strong stand when the big issues come up, and compromising on the lesser ones. A passive approach might work when assertiveness would be wasted on somebody who's too preoccupied to notice you or too powerless to respond. Let it go until both sides will be all there and ready to listen. Aggression, on the other hand, is useful in a crisis, particularly when you must take drastic action to protect yourself either physically or emotionally. Trickiest of all is indirect aggression (see Chapter 14 for a full discussion of manipulation). If you know what you're doing, it might be effective when applied sparingly — but never as a long-term strategy.

When you write about "the Compassion Trap," it sounds as if you think compassion is bad. Why? Although we didn't invent the phrase (Margaret Adams did, in a 1971 article), we recognized "the Compassion Trap" instantly. It describes the woman who believes she has no choice but to put all her energy into taking care of other people, regardless of her own needs. Compassion — a deep awareness of the suffering of another, coupled by the desire to relieve it — is only a trap when it enslaves. To feel compassion is to be human. We do not suggest that the assertive woman put her heart in the deep freeze. Real compassion, however, springs from an equally deep self-respect first. It is being sensitive to (but not enslaved by) another's feelings.

You say assertiveness is a plus, but aren't there minuses as well? What about the cost of assertiveness? In the beginning, naysayers claimed that assertive women would singlehandedly destroy the American family and every other tradition that our society holds dear. That, of course, was (and is) ridiculous, but the piper must be paid: having more *freedom* to choose carries more *responsibility* to live with the results, which won't always be easy. Deciding, for instance, to put off starting a family may be a smart career move, but Mother Nature's already done the math; a woman's body doesn't care one bit that she's made an assertive choice. The physical cost (or benefit) will be felt later, when she comes face to face with the impact of her decision.

Psychology is important too. Although assertiveness is increasingly rewarded in women, there remains a not-so-subtle expectation that she ought to remember her (submissive) place. When she bucks this trend, she steps out, a gain that won't always be applauded. If this happens in significant relationships, they must be rebuilt on a more equitable footing, or the cost may be the loss of the relationship itself.

Most of the time, though, the benefits of assertiveness ---- self-esteem, confidence, enthusiasm, energy ---- are contagious and far outdistance the costs. Most of us find ways to integrate assertiveness into our lives without sparking a crisis, and in such a way that the people we care the most about back us up. In other words, it's an evolution, not a revolution.

Assertiveness isn't for women only, is it? Don't men need to learn how to be assertive, too? Lots of people have asked us why we didn't just call this book *The Assertive Person*, since the ability to assert oneself is an equal opportunity skill and an attractive trait to boot ---- in men and women. But back in 1975, assertive women were overwhelming and threatening. Their presence suggested that traditional, eager-to-please girlishness would be thrown over for a grown-up femininity. An assertive woman would be fully capable of making her own choices, and would not feel compelled to get anyone's permission first. An assertive woman could look you in the eye and tell you she liked you ---- attractive in a man, but in a woman, disconcerting in the extreme.

Even now, two decades later, it's somehow easier, to accept assertiveness as an essentially masculine quality. There's room for a book called *The Assertive Woman!* (Several good books on assertiveness are intended for both men and women readers.) Because women had gotten used to denying the validity of their own thoughts, feelings and talent, we wrote for them. We hoped they would respond as we did, that it was such a relief to know you weren't alone, that your feelings deserved respect, that you didn't have to go through life as somebody's old doormat, that asserting yourself didn't mean locking out of your life the people you cared about the most. We think the world could use more assertiveness from men *and* women, although our closest bond is still with women. Their experiences, after all, mirror our own.

Chapter 24

Same Song, Third Verse

I've always wanted to be somebody. But I see now I should have been more specific.

~~ Lily Tomlin

Looking back now, it seems obvious that the original publication of *The Assertive Woman* in 1975 came at the beginning of a transformation in the lives of women that would change the world forever. "Two hundred years ago," in the words of writer Shannon Brownlee, "women took a back seat to their fathers, husbands, and sons; the closest they could come to power was marrying it. Then, in a tenth of the time it took to build the nation, not one but two women took their seats on the U.S. Supreme Court."

Now assertive women have advanced to lofty positions nearly everywhere: they run companies, head churches, lend their names to ships (the "U.S.S. Hopper") and shoes (Nike's Air Swoopes), enforce laws, guard the Tomb of the Unknown Soldier at Arlington, edit *The Wall Street Journal*, appear on Wheaties boxes, fly the space shuttle and captain starships on TV.

When Barbara Walters was asked how she's stayed on top of broadcast journalism for four decades, she replied, "All I know is that I kept going." Like Walters, assertive women persist. Let's applaud them for conquering every barrier that stood in their way as they fought to enter classrooms and boardrooms and locker rooms. Look what they've changed, in just the blink of an eye:

In 1976, women held only 2 percent of all patents, but thanks to inventors like chemist Agnes McQueary (who developed Bounce and Downy fabric softeners) and Dr. Patricia Bath, who came up with a device for removing cataracts, women now receive 8 percent of the roughly 100,000 patents awarded annually. In Canada, women-led firms are creating jobs at four times the national average and increasing in number at double the national average, figures that closely mirror those in the United States. Women now comprise some 13.5 percent of the U.S. armed forces. Between the Montreal Olympics in 1976 and the Summer Games in Atlanta in 1996, the number of female athletes competing for the American team more than doubled, from 133 to 297. Women are a $2.3 trillion market, own 43 percent of stock portfolios over $50,000, and account for over half of all consumer purchases in almost all consumer categories. Since 1995, Carol Gelet has coached the winning Clairton High's *boys'* basketball team in Pennsylvania. In a 1996 survey about success and leadership commissioned by the Sara Lee Corporation, respondents were asked what their daughters should aspire to; 28 percent said "CEO of a Fortune 500 company;" the same percentage chose "winning a Nobel Prize."

If you want to see what the next twenty ---- or two hundred ---- years have in store, you won't have to wait for a formal survey. Ask a young woman who was born twenty or even ten years ago what she plans to do with her life. Win that Nobel Prize? Or race cars and set speed records or design software or be President or fly airplanes or a zillion other things? One thing's for sure, thanks to the changes we've ignited these past two decades, she won't have to take a back seat to anyone.

The Assertive Woman has helped thousands of women find and use their voices in this fast-moving world of ours. If it weren't for women with guts and brains, the Family and Medical Leave Act would never have passed, 81 percent of Fortune 500 companies would not have at least one female director, and Congress would never have agreed to move the monument to early suffragists out of the Capitol basement and into the Rotunda. No question, there are still plenty of launch windows for change. Here are some that could use a few assertive women:

- Work on or run a political campaign.
- Run for city council, a school board seat, the House of Representatives, a Senate seat ...
- Vote.
- Stand up for a cause you believe in.

• Assist public schools in developing alternative teaching methods to help girls succeed in math and science.

• Push corporate employers to expand benefits programs to include "family-friendly" policies. Some to consider are day care, parental leave, flextime, a bring-kids-to-work option, telecommuting, a company cafeteria that makes up take-home and low-fat meals.

• If employees are being sexually harassed at your place of work, report it. Do not tolerate it.

• Find out how you can get involved with the three global concerns that affect the long-term security and well-being of all people as we enter a new century: health, population and the environment.

• Support the public recognition of women's achievements with a national holiday that commemorates a famous woman (so far, all the national birthdays are men's).

• Bring your daughters (or niece, or sister) to work.

• Keep up with the help of technology: get online and meet women from all over the world through Women's Wire, a superb Internet web site (http://www.women.com), and you can tap into other women-oriented web sites through the Directory of Women-Oriented Sites (http://www.bizwomen.com/links/woriented.html

Assertiveness is more than the communication aid it used to be. As the roster above shows, it's a way to lay the groundwork for a whole new generation of women who will make their mark in the world. To be an assertive woman is to contribute to society by investing yourself in a venture that is worthy of your passion and courage: helping girls grow strong, guiding a company, keeping a home, running a government. What a difference a couple of decades makes!

The revolution that began twenty years ago isn't over yet. Where will it take you?

Index

MORE BOOKS WITH *IMPACT*

We think you will find these Impact Publishers titles of interest:

YOUR PERFECT RIGHT
A Guide to Assertive Living (Seventh Edition)
Robert E. Alberti, Ph.D., & Michael L. Emmons, Ph.D.
Softcover: $12.95   Hardcover: $17.95   256pp.
Twenty-fifth Anniversary Edition of the assertiveness book most recommended by psychologists — fifth most recommended among all self-help books!

REBUILDING
When Your Relationship Ends (Second Edition)
Bruce Fisher, Ed.D.
Softcover: $11.95   336pp.
The most popular guide to divorce recovery. The "divorce process rebuilding blocks" format offers a nineteen-step process for putting life back together after divorce. More than half a million in print.

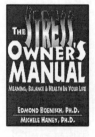

THE STRESS OWNER'S MANUAL
Meaning, Balance and Health in Your Life
Ed Boenisch, Ph.D., and Michele Haney, Ph.D.
Softcover: $12.95   208pp.
Practical guide to stress management with self-assessment charts covering people, money, work, leisure stress areas. Life-changing strategies to enhance relaxation and serenity.

EVERY SESSION COUNTS
Making the Most of Your Brief Therapy
John Preston, Psy.D.
Softcover: $9.95   128pp.
Tight-budget times demand short-term, cost effective procedures. This excellent guide helps you make the most of brief therapy.

Impact 🕮 Publishers®
POST OFFICE BOX 1094
SAN LUIS OBISPO, CALIFORNIA 93406

Please see the following page for more books.